ROBERT D. BEZUCHA
PROJECT DIRECTOR

NORMAN F. GUESS
EDITORIAL DIRECTOR

R. JAMES ERTEL
MANAGING EDITOR

ALICE F. MARTIN
ASSOCIATE EDITOR

GENEVIEVE CURLEY
JOAN FALK

PAULINE NORTON
ASSISTANT PROJECT DIRECTOR

RICHARD D. HARKINS
HESTER GELB

CONTRIBUTORS AND CONSULTANTS

Hall Bartlett, Ed.D., Citizenship Education Project, Teachers College, Columbia University; Author

Walt Disney, Motion Picture and Television Producer

Evelyn Millis Duvall, Ph.D., Author and Consultant on Family Life; Authority on Child Development

Edna E. Eisen, Ph.D., Professor of Geography, Kent State University

J. Allen Hynek, Ph.D., Associate Director, Smithsonian Astrophysical Observatory

Leland B. Jacobs, Ph.D., Professor of Education, Teachers College, Columbia University

Eleanor M. Johnson, M.A., Director of Elementary School Services, Graduate Division, Wesleyan University

Herbert A. Landry, M.S., Ph.D., Director, Bureau of Educational Program Research and Statistics, New York City Public Schools

Milton Levine, M.D., Associate Professor of Pediatrics, New York Hospital

Willy Ley, Professor of Science, Fairleigh Dickinson University; Rocket Expert and Author

Norman Lloyd, M.A., Teacher of Literature and Materials of Music, Juilliard School of Music

Lenox R. Lohr, M.E., D.Eng., D.Sc., President, Museum of Science and Industry, Chicago

Will C. McKern, D.S., Former Director, Milwaukee Public Museum; Anthropologist

Richard A. Martin, B.S., Curator, N. W. Harris Public School Extension, Chicago Natural History Museum

Maurice Pate, Executive Director, United Nations Children's Fund (UNICEF)

Norman Vincent Peale, D.D., LL.D., Litt.D., LH.D.; Minister, Marble Collegiate Church, New York; Author

Rutherford Platt, B.A., Member of Two North Pole Expeditions with Admiral MacMillan; Author of Nature Books

Illa Podendorf, M.S., Teacher of Science, University of Chicago Laboratory Schools; Author of Science Books

Mary M. Reed, Ph.D., Supervisor of Little Golden Books; Formerly of Teachers College, Columbia University

John R. Saunders, M.A., Chairman, Department of Public Instruction, American Museum of Natural History

Glenn T. Seaborg, Ph.D., LL.D., D.Sc., Chancellor and Professor of Chemistry, University of California, Berkeley; Associate Director, University of California Radiation Laboratory; Co-winner of Nobel Prize for Chemistry, 1951

Louis Shores, Ph.D., Dean of the Library School, Florida State University; Author and Authority on Reference Materials

Nila Banton Smith, Ph.B., Ph.D., Professor of Education and Director of The Reading Institute, New York University

Bryan Swan, M.S., Teacher of Physical Science, University of Chicago Laboratory Schools; Author

Samuel Terrien, S.T.M., Th.D., Auburn Professor of the Old Testament, Union Theological Seminary

Jessie Todd, M.A., Formerly of the Art Department, University of Chicago; Art Lecturer; Contributor to Art Magazines

Lloyd B. Urdal, Ph.D., Assistant Professor, School of Education, State College of Washington

Jane Werner Watson, B.A., Editor and Author of More Than a Hundred Golden Books

William S. Weichert, M.S., Supervisor of Science, Oakland (Calif.) Public Schools

Paul A. Witty, Ph.D., Professor of Education, Northwestern University; Specialist on Gifted Children

THE
GOLDEN BOOK
ENCYCLOPEDIA

VOLUME XII—PARICUTIN TO QUICKSAND

In Sixteen Accurate, Fact-filled Volumes Dramatically Illustrated
with More Than 6,000 Color Pictures

THE ONLY ENCYCLOPEDIA FOR YOUNG GRADE-SCHOOL CHILDREN

ACCURATE AND AUTHORITATIVE

ENTERTAININGLY WRITTEN AND ILLUSTRATED TO
MAKE LEARNING AN ADVENTURE

by Bertha Morris Parker

Formerly of the Laboratory Schools, University of Chicago
Research Associate, Chicago Natural History Museum

GOLDEN PRESS · NEW YORK

Paricutín started in a cornfield and in eight months had grown to 1500 feet.

PARICUTÍN (pa ree koo TEEN) There are hundreds of live volcanoes in the world, but only one could have a birthday party. There is only one volcano whose birthday we know—Paricutín, in Mexico. Its birthday is February 20.

On February 20, 1943, a Mexican farmer was plowing his cornfield. His small son was with him. The boy came running to his father to say that he had heard a noise under the ground. The farmer had been shouting to his ox and had not heard the noise. When he stopped to listen, he heard what sounded like a deep growl. At first he saw nothing strange. Then he noticed a cloud of smoke coming out of a small opening in the ground. He hurried back to his home in the village to get his wife and the priest and the neighbors. When they reached the cornfield, they found the beginnings of a volcano.

In the days and weeks that followed, chunks of rock were hurled high into the air in a series of explosions. Ashes were shot upwards thousands of feet. Soon all the region round about was covered with a layer of ash. After several weeks lava began to pour from the volcano's crater. In four months the volcano built itself into a cone 1,000 feet tall.

When the volcano was a year old, it was 1,500 feet high. The village of Paricutín near by was now almost buried in ashes. The people in the village had had to move away. Another small village near by was abandoned, too. All the pine forests in the region were dead. The fields were deep in ashes. Ashes and lava were still coming from the volcano, and dark clouds hovered over it. There were often flashes of lightning in these clouds. They glowed red from the hot rock below, too. Sometimes there was a great rumbling or roaring.

When Paricutín was five years old, it was showing signs of dying down. Not so much lava and not so many ashes were pouring out. At last the eruptions stopped altogether. Probably Paricutín will never be any higher. And probably it has done all the damage it will ever do. But no one can ever be sure that a volcano will stay dead. (See MOUNTAINS; VOLCANOES.)

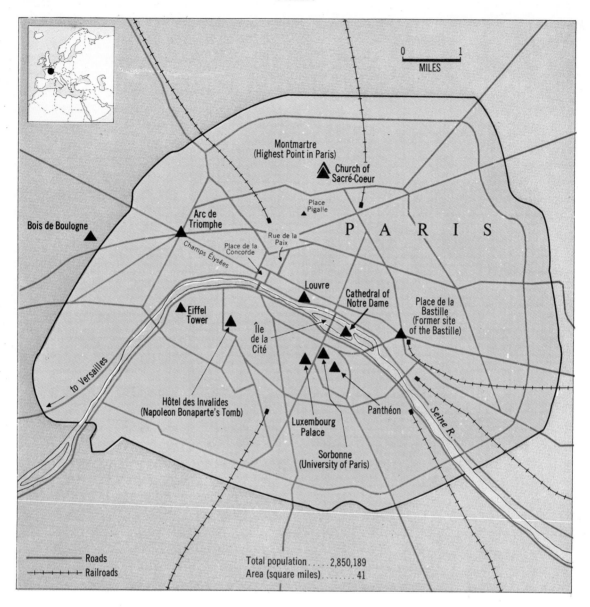

Montmartre
(Highest Point in Paris)

Church of
Sacré-Coeur

Place
Pigalle

P A R I S

Arc de
Triomphe

Bois de Boulogne

Rue de la
Paix

Champs Élysées

Place de la
Concorde

Louvre

Eiffel
Tower

Cathedral of
Notre Dame

Place de la
Bastille
(Former site
of the Bastille)

Île
de la
Cité

to Versailles

Panthéon

Seine R.

Hôtel des Invalides
(Napoleon Bonaparte's Tomb)

Luxembourg
Palace

Sorbonne
(University of Paris)

0   1
MILES

——— Roads
+++++ Railroads

Total population......2,850,189
Area (square miles)........41

Policeman

The Opéra

Sidewalk Cafe

Luxembourg Gardens

PARIS Every year a great many visitors go to Paris, the capital of France. Its beauty and gaiety make people want to see it. Besides, it has many historic treasures. It is also a leader in art and music, and is one of the fashion centers of the world.

In 1889 Paris held a World's Fair. The Eiffel Tower, 984 feet high, was built for that fair. It still stands. Visitors often go to the top of this tower to view Paris. They see below them the river Seine flowing through the city. On both sides of the river stand handsome government buildings. In the river lies a boat-shaped island. Here about 2,000 years ago Paris began as a little fishing village. On the island a big cathedral now stands out clearly. It is Notre Dame, one of the world's most famous churches.

The fishing village was in a good place for growing. Boats could easily come up and down the river to it. The village soon spread to the banks of the river. Then roads could reach it from all directions. In time the village became a walled city. Some of the beautiful boulevards seen in looking down on the city are where the old walls once stood.

In Paris there are no skyscrapers like those of American cities. But above the treetops rise the roofs and towers of royal palaces, ancient and modern universities, museums, theaters, and churches. They are reminders that Paris for many centuries was the most powerful and cultured city in Europe. Around the horizon runs a circle of green hills. In earlier times they helped protect Paris from invaders.

Paris has beautiful formal gardens. In one of these, the Luxembourg Gardens, there is a small pool. By the pool one usually finds many children. They enjoy rolling big hoops around the pool or sailing toy boats across its waters.

As they walk along the streets, visitors see many signs that Paris is a center of fashion. The streets are crowded with shops where dresses, hats, gloves, shoes, purses, and jewelry are sold. Sidewalk cafes make the streets attractive.

Hundreds of thousands of the people of Paris work in factories. But most of the factories manufacture rather small things that take much skill to make. There is no coal near by; it must all be shipped in. It would not pay, therefore, to make heavy machinery. Some farm machines and automobiles are made, but many factories make such things as fine paper, surgical instruments, perfumes, and leather goods.

Roads, railroads, and airlines lead to Paris from all over France. They tie the many sections of France to its capital city. Wharves line both sides of the river. Paris is about 100 miles from the sea, but tons of such things as oil, wheat, and coal come up to it from the ocean port of Le Havre. It is not strange that Paris is the largest city of France as well as the capital. About 3,000,000 people live there.

The people of other cities in the world are pleased whenever they are told that their city is like Paris. Being like Paris, as we have seen, means being a city of beauty, a city of pleasure, a fashion center, a center of art and learning, and a great industrial city all rolled into one. (See EIFFEL TOWER; FRANCE.)

Eiffel Tower

Obelisk in the *Place de la Concorde*

Fisherman by the Seine

PARROTS AND PARAKEETS

PARROTS AND PARAKEETS Many birds can sing, but only a few can talk. The best talkers are parrots and parakeets.

When parrots and parakeets talk, they do not know what they are saying. They are merely saying something they have heard over and over again. They are good mimics. They may mimic other sounds besides talking—such sounds as the barking of a dog, the mewing of a cat, or the crying of a baby.

There are several hundred kinds of parrots and parakeets. In size they go all the way from the pygmy parrot of New Guinea, which is only three inches long, to the black cockatoo of Australia, which is a yard long. Some have truly beautiful colors.

All parrots and parakeets are alike in a number of ways. They have rather stout bodies. Their bills are strong and hooked. On each of their feet two toes point forward and two backward. With their feet they can walk, perch, and climb. They can also hold food with their feet.

Many parrots used to be taught to say "Polly wants a cracker." Really there are many things that parrots and parakeets would rather have than crackers. Crackers alone would not keep them healthy, either. When they are in their native lands they eat chiefly seeds and fruits. One kind of parrot in Australia, however, kills sheep and eats them.

Most parrots and parakeets live in warm lands. Only one kind has ever been common as a wild bird in the United States. This is the Carolina parakeet. During the early days of the United States this bird was common in the Carolinas and southward. There were great flocks of parakeets. They nested in trees and sometimes annoyed people with their harsh calls. Now this bird has disappeared. If any at all are left they are hidden in the forests of Florida.

The parrots most often kept as pets are the African gray parrot and the Amazon parrot. Sailors used to bring many of these birds home from their ocean voyages. These two parrots have better dispositions than most of the other big parrots. But not even these parrots are very popular now. Some of the little parrots and parakeets are much more popular.

The little Australian lovebird is the most popular parakeet. Another name for it is budgerigar (BUJ er e gar). Its nickname is "budgie." Budgies make excellent pets. They are beautiful and are easy to take care of. With patience they can be taught to say many words, and even whole phrases.

Parrots are long-lived. Big parrots may live to be 50 years old or even older. (See BIRDS; PETS.)

PARTNERSHIPS AMONG LIVING THINGS

PARTNERSHIPS AMONG LIVING THINGS A field of red clover is a good place to look for bumblebees. Bumblebees get nectar for honey from the clover blossoms. As the bees go about getting nectar they carry pollen from blossom to blossom. The pollen is needed to make clover seed form. The bees, therefore, are helping the clover by carrying pollen, and the clover is helping the bees by giving them nectar.

Clover plants and bumblebees are good partners. Apple trees and honey bees help each other just as bumblebees and clover do.

Yucca moths and yucca plants are good partners in much the same way. Yucca moths carry pollen from blossom to blossom and help seeds form. They lay eggs in the yucca flowers, and the baby moths eat some of the seeds. Without yucca plants there could be no yucca moths, and without yucca moths there could be no seeds to start new yucca plants.

In a partnership the partners may be a plant and an animal. But the partners may both be animals, or they may both be plants.

Ants and aphids are animal partners. Aphids suck the juices of plants. They get more sugar than they need and give off drops of a sweet liquid called honeydew. Ants eat the honeydew. In return the ants take care of the aphids. They keep them in the ant nests during the winter. They protect them from their enemies. And they carry the aphids to fresh young plants.

Another animal-animal partnership is made up of wood-eating cockroaches and tiny one-celled animals called protozoa. The protozoa live inside the cockroaches. The cockroaches eat wood, but they cannot digest it. The protozoa digest it for them. In return the cockroaches give the protozoa food and a safe home.

Orchids and fungi are plant partners. The fungi get food from the orchid plants. In return they help the orchids get water, and they help orchid seeds start to grow.

Bee Pollinating an Apple Blossom

Lichens are among the best of all partnerships. Every lichen is really two kinds of plants in one—green algae and colorless fungi. The algae make food for themselves and for the fungi. The fungi take in water for themselves and for the algae.

There are many, many other partnerships among living things. But when we see two plants or two animals or a plant and an animal living together, we cannot be sure that they are really partners. One may be doing a great deal of harm to the other. Aphids on a young nasturtium plant are getting all their food from the plant. But they are not helping the plant in any way. They may even kill it. (See ANTS; LICHENS; ORCHIDS; POLLINATION.)

The night-blooming yucca plant depends on the yucca moth for life. Without the yucca moth there could be no new plants, nor could the baby moth live without the food it gets from the yucca plant.

PASSENGER PIGEON Less than 100 years ago passenger pigeons were common all over eastern North America. They roosted together in great colonies and flew together in huge flocks. They flew in such big flocks that sometimes the sun was hidden from view for an hour at a time.

Now there is not a passenger pigeon in North America or anywhere else in the world. This bird has become extinct.

Matilda, the last living passenger pigeon, died September 1, 1914. She was hatched in the Cincinnati zoo and lived her whole life there. She died at the age of 26. The man who took care of Matilda tried hard to find a mate for her so that he might raise more passenger pigeons, but he was never able to find one.

Passenger pigeons became extinct because so many of them were killed for food. It was easy to kill or catch a great many at a time. Trees could be found that had more than 100 nests in them. Nesting birds were easily caught. And pigeons would gather close together if grain were scattered for them. Many could then be shot or caught in nets. Sometimes more than 200 dozen were taken in one catch. The last big catch was in Michigan in 1878.

Passenger pigeons were very much like their relatives, the mourning doves. But they were bigger. Of course, there is no way of getting them back again. (See BIRDS OF YESTERDAY; CONSERVATION.)

PASSION PLAY In 1633 there was a great plague in Europe. Many thousands of people died of it. But some places escaped the plague. One of them was the small village of Oberammergau in southern Germany. The people of this village wanted to show how thankful they were for having been spared. They decided to give a play telling the story of the life of Jesus.

This play became famous. It was called the Passion play. Every ten years the people of the village gave the play. There were 350 parts in it, and the villagers themselves took all the parts. It was a great honor to be chosen for some roles. The play became so famous that people came from all over the world to see it.

The Passion play of Oberammergau was not performed during World War II, but it was resumed in 1950. Other Passion plays are given in other places. One, for instance, is given every summer in Spearfish, South Dakota. (See JESUS.)

PASTEUR, LOUIS (1822-1895) A hundred years ago no one knew that bacteria, tiny plants too small to be seen without a microscope, are the cause of many diseases. No one knew that these tiny plants, by spreading from one person to another, can cause terrible epidemics. It was Louis Pasteur, a French chemist, who proved that some bacteria are disease germs and who showed that scientists can find ways of preventing germ diseases. He also developed pasteurization.

Pasteur was already a famous scientist when a dreadful disease of animals called "anthrax" began to spread rapidly on the farms of France. Cattle and sheep were dying by the thousands. The French government asked for Pasteur's help. A few scientists had found bacteria in the bodies of animals that had died of anthrax, and some of these scientists had suspected that the bacteria were the cause of the disease. Most people, however, thought that the idea was foolish. They could not believe that anything so tiny could kill animals as big as sheep and cows.

Pasteur, too, found bacteria in the bodies of animals that had died of anthrax. He was able to grow these bacteria in test tubes in such a way that they were very weak. He tried putting weak bacteria into the body of a healthy animal and later putting strong bacteria into the body of the same animal. The animal did not get sick even though around it other animals died of anthrax.

Many people still refused to believe that sheep so treated would not catch anthrax. To prove that he was right, Pasteur began a public experiment on 50 healthy sheep. He put some weak anthrax germs into the bodies of 25 of the sheep. Two weeks after that, strong anthrax germs were put into the bodies of all 50 sheep. Pasteur predicted that the 25 sheep that had first been given the weak germs would stay well and that the other 25 would die. Two days later a great crowd gathered in the pasture to see how the experiment would turn out. Just as Pasteur predicted, 25 sheep were dead; the 25 that had first been given weak germs were grazing peacefully. Pasteur had shown a way to fight anthrax.

Pasteur later found a way to keep people who were bitten by mad dogs from getting the disease called "hydrophobia," or "rabies." He had successfully tried out his method of treatment on animals, but for a long time he was afraid to try it on people. Then one day a little boy who had been badly bitten by a mad dog was brought to Pasteur. Hydrophobia and death for the boy were almost a certainty. A worried Pasteur began the treatment. Each day for 12 days stronger and stronger germs were put into the boy's body. Pasteur slept little. But the boy stayed well. At last Pasteur knew that his treatment was a success.

Pasteur was born in Dôle, France, the son of a tanner. His parents, though hardworking, were poor. They struggled to give their son a good education, never dreaming that he would one day be the greatest scientist in France. Before his death the people of France paid him many honors. Seven years before he died, they erected a great building with many laboratories and called it Pasteur Institute. In it numerous scientists carry on the work Pasteur began. (See BACTERIA; DISEASE GERMS; DISEASES; FRANCE.)

Pasteur revolutionized men's ideas about disease by proving that many diseases are caused by germs.

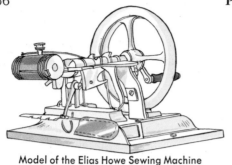

Model of the Elias Howe Sewing Machine

PATENTS "Patent No. 2312142." "Patent Pending." "Patent Applied For." We see such phrases on many of the things we buy and use. They are signs that the United States Government protects inventors. A patent gives the inventor the sole right to make and sell his invention for 17 years. No one is allowed to copy his idea during that time without paying him. Other countries issue patents, too.

The story of Samuel Crompton shows why patents are needed. Crompton was an English weaver who lived at the time the American colonies were forming a new nation. In those days all weaving was done by hand. Crompton lived with his widowed mother and a crippled uncle in an old mansion on the edge of a wood. His loom stood in the corner of the living room. The family was poor. As a boy Samuel had had to learn to weave as soon as he was strong enough to work the loom.

As he worked his loom Crompton had to stop every few minutes because his thread broke. How wonderful it would be, he thought, if he could find a way of spinning a stronger thread. For five years he experimented. He worked in secret. At last he had a machine that would spin fine, strong thread, or yarn. He wove the new yarn into muslin. His was the best yarn of the kind that had ever been spun.

Of course, other weavers wanted to have this better yarn to use. They came to Crompton to buy it. Soon Crompton spent all his time spinning. And soon other spinners had a hard time selling their yarn.

Crompton would not let anyone see his machine. He was afraid others would build machines like it, and he would lose his trade in yarn. He thought he deserved some reward for his long years of work. The other spinners threatened to break into his house and wreck his machine. They were afraid they would soon not be able to earn a living. Of course, as long as Crompton kept his invention a secret, only a few of the people of England had a chance to buy really good muslin.

There were patents in England in those days, but it was hard for a poor inventor to get one. At last Crompton agreed to let some manufacturers copy his machine. The manufacturers did not keep their word about the amount of money they would pay him. Crompton received very little.

Before long the invention was being used all over England. The government saw that Crompton had not had a fair reward for his work. They gave him 5,000 pounds. If Crompton had had a patent, he would not have been afraid to show his machine. No one would have been able to use his invention without paying him for the privilege.

In the United States Constitution the government was given the right to issue patents. The builders of the country knew that the world needs inventions and that inventors must be encouraged.

In the nation's first year only three patents were issued. The very first one was given to Samuel Hopkins of Vermont. He had invented a new way of getting lye for soap from wood ashes. Today the United States Patent Office issues tens of thousands of patents a year. It has issued more than 2,500,000 altogether.

An inventor who wants to patent a new invention first sends in a description of his invention to the Patent Office. He signs papers to say that the invention is his own idea. He pays a small fee. Workers in the Patent Office study the invention. If they decide that it is something really new, the inventor pays another fee. Then the Patent Office issues the patent.

Until 1880 the Patent Office required that a model of the invention be sent in. The picture shows one such model. Many models are now in the Patent Office or in the National Museum.

Not all inventions turn out to be useful. But many are so useful that they have made large fortunes for their inventors. (See INVENTIONS.)

PATRIOTIC SONGS Every country has its patriotic songs. And almost every country has its official national anthem. The national anthem of the United States is "The Star-Spangled Banner."

Francis Scott Key wrote the words for "The Star-Spangled Banner" in 1814, during the War of 1812 between the Americans and the British. A friend of Key's was being held a prisoner on the British ship "Surprise" in Chesapeake Bay. The president of the United States gave Key permission to ask the British for his friend's release. Soon after Key boarded the "Surprise," the ship received orders to bombard Fort McHenry, near Baltimore. Key had to stay on the ship. All night he listened to the loud bombardment and wondered whether the Americans would surrender.

When morning came, Key saw that the American flag was still flying over the fort. It was then that he wrote the words of the famous song. Soon the words were being sung to an old English tune. In 1931 "The Star-Spangled Banner" became the official national anthem of the United States.

"America" is a well-known patriotic song of the United States. The words were written in 1832 by the Reverend Samuel F. Smith. No one knows who wrote the music. To the same tune the British sing their national anthem, "God Save the King."

"America the Beautiful" is another patriotic song of America. Katharine Lee Bates wrote the words after looking out over the countryside from the top of Pikes Peak.

"Yankee Doodle" has been a patriotic song in America since before the Revolutionary War. "Hail Columbia" was written by Joseph Hopkinson in 1798, when there seemed to be danger that the young United States would have to take part in a war between France and England.

"The Battle Cry of Freedom," "Marching through Georgia," "When Johnny Comes Marching Home," "John Brown's Body," and "Dixie" were songs sung during the War between the States. "Dixie," the chief war song of the South, was written by Daniel Emmett, a Northerner. Just as the North gave "Dixie" to the South, the South gave the North "John Brown's Body" or "Glory Hallelujah." Julia Ward Howe in 1861 wrote new words for the tune. She named the song "The Battle Hymn of the Republic." Three of the most popular war songs of World War I were "Over There," "Keep the Home Fires Burning," and "There's a Long, Long Trail."

Among the patriotic songs of other countries are the following:

Belgium—"La Brabanconne"
Canada—"O Canada"
　　　　 "The Maple Leaf Forever"
Denmark—"King Christian Stood Beside the Mast"
Finland—"Our Land"
France—"La Marseillaise"
Italy—"Royal Italian March"
　　　 "Come, Arise Ye"
Norway—"Song for Norway"
Soviet Union—"Hymn to the Soviet Union"
Sweden—"From the Depths of Swedish Hearts"
Switzerland—"To the Fatherland"

(See BALTIMORE; UNITED STATES HISTORY; YANKEE DOODLE.)

THE STAR SPANGLED BANNER

American patriots rebelled against the English.

PATRIOTS Some 600 years ago, an old story goes, a village in Switzerland was ruled by a cruel Austrian governor. One day he put his hat on a pole in the village square and ordered everyone who passed to bow down to it. William Tell, a villager, refused to bow down. He and his young son were brought before the governor. To punish him, the governor ordered his soldiers to put an apple on the son's head. Then he ordered William Tell to shoot the apple off the boy's head.

Tell succeeded in shooting off the apple without harming his son. Just as he and the boy were about to leave, the governor saw that Tell had another arrow under his belt. "What were you going to do with it?" the governor asked.

"I was going to kill you, too," answered Tell, "if I had killed my son."

Of course, Tell then had to flee for his life. Later he helped his countrymen win their freedom from Austria.

For a long time people thought that this story was true. But now they are sure it is not. There are stories almost exactly like it in the legends of several other countries.

There are many true stories of people who have showed great bravery in helping their country. We call such people patriots.

The people of South America would probably call Simón Bolívar their greatest patriot. He helped them free themselves from Spain. Giuseppe Garibaldi was a

great Italian patriot. He helped bring all Italy and Sicily together into one country. The great Polish patriot, Thaddeus Kosciusko (kos e US ko), led the Poles in their fight to free themselves from Russian rule. Robert Bruce led the Scots in their fight for freedom. Joan of Arc saved the French throne for her king. The list could go on and on. Every country has its patriots.

A person does not actually have to fight to be a patriot. All the men who signed the Declaration of Independence were risking their lives. If the colonies had not won their freedom, these men might all have been killed as traitors.

Among the signers of the Declaration of Independence were such patriots as John Adams, Samuel Adams, Benjamin Franklin, John Hancock, Thomas Jefferson, and Robert Morris. One name in the list of signers has a place name after it—Charles Carroll of Carrollton. First Carroll signed just his name; then someone pointed out that he was in less danger than the others because there were so many Charles Carrolls. At once Carroll added "of Carrollton" so that there could be no mistake about which Carroll had signed.

There have been many more great patriots since the Declaration of Independence was signed. In World War I and World War II millions of Americans showed their patriotism. Many did it by fighting. Others did their work "behind the scenes."

The Americans were proud of their new flag.

PEARL HARBOR

PEARL HARBOR The American naval base of Pearl Harbor is in the Hawaiian Islands. It is one of the best and largest in the world. Many ships can anchor in the harbor. Vessels can be repaired in the big dry docks. There is a special base for submarines. The "Nautilus" started from Pearl Harbor on its famous trip under the ice at the North Pole. On an island in the harbor there is an air base.

The Japanese attacked Pearl Harbor on December 7, 1941. This attack brought the United States into World War II.

PEARLS Most precious stones are found in rocks. But pearls are not. They are found inside the shells of oysters and other shellfish. Most of them come from a kind of oyster called the pearl oyster.

A pearl oyster makes a pearl in this way: Something tiny finds its way inside the oyster's shell. It may be a grain of sand or a tiny worm. To keep it from doing any harm, the oyster builds a wall around it. The oyster uses the same material it lines its shell with. It puts on one layer after another. After a while the grain of sand or worm has been wrapped up in so many layers that it is a beautiful little ball—a pearl.

Once in a while a pearl grows to be very large. The largest one that has ever been found came from a giant clam. This big pearl weighed 14 pounds.

The best pearls are those that come from the Persian Gulf. Many Arabs make a living by diving for them.

An Arab pearl diver dives from a boat. Usually there are many other divers on the boat with him. Each diver has a helper. For his dive he needs a heavy ball on the end of a rope, a light basket on the end of a rope, and a sharp knife. He may also want a clothespin to put on his nose.

The heavy ball carries him to the bottom of the water—perhaps 50 or 60 feet down. He fills the basket as fast as he can. If a shark comes near, he protects himself with his knife.

As soon as his basket is full, his helper pulls it up. His helper may pull him up, too, or he may swim up by himself. As soon as he reaches the boat, he dumps out the oysters and opens them, hoping that there will be at least one pearl.

Some years ago the Japanese found that they could "plant" grains of sand inside oyster shells and produce pearls in this way. Such pearls are called cultured pearls. Pearls that grow naturally bring higher prices. (See BIRTHSTONES; DIVING; MOLLUSKS; OYSTERS.)

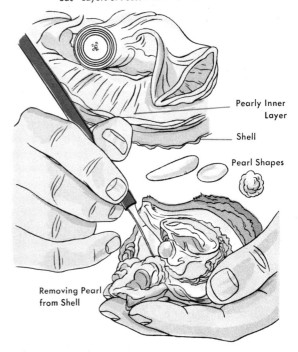

Sac Layers of Pearl Particles

Pearly Inner Layer

Shell

Pearl Shapes

Removing Pearl from Shell

Huskies pulled the sledges to the Pole.

PEARY, ROBERT E. (1856-1920) Early in July in 1908 an American explorer sailed from New York City to find the North Pole. He was Robert E. Peary. His boat was named the "Roosevelt."

For two months Peary and his men traveled northward. At last they reached an island about 450 miles from the North Pole. They decided to spend the winter on their boat near the shore of the island. The long arctic night was about to begin.

It was very, very cold. Soon the "Roosevelt" was frozen in the ice. Before long blizzards almost buried the boat in snow.

For several days every month there was moonlight. On these days some of the men went hunting. They caught musk oxen and seals and polar bears. The fresh meat helped keep the men well.

A few days before the end of February Peary and most of his men left the boat. They traveled along the shore of the island until they reached its northernmost point. From here, on the first day of March, they started across the Arctic Ocean toward the Pole. They carried their food and fuel on sledges. Eskimo dogs pulled the sledges.

The ocean was mostly frozen. But there were, here and there, lanes of open water. When the men reached one of these lanes they had to wait patiently. Before many days it was sure either to close up or to freeze over. At night the men built snow houses for themselves and their dogs.

Going was slow even when there were no lanes of water. There were many storms, and the ice was very rough. The party kept growing smaller, for as soon as a sledge was empty the driver and his dogs started back to the boat. At last Peary had with him only one Negro, four Eskimos, and 38 dogs. With them he reached the Pole.

Of course, there was no pole sticking up in the ice to tell where the North Pole was. Peary had to study the sun to find out when he had reached the Pole. He made other measurements, too.

It was April 6 when Peary decided from his measurements that he was at the Pole. He planted an American flag in the ice there. In his diary he wrote, "The Pole at last. The prize of three centuries. My dream and goal for 20 years."

By September Peary and his men were safely home. When he showed his records, scientists agreed that he had really reached the North Pole. In *The North Pole,* published in 1910, Peary told of his trip. (See ARCTIC OCEAN; ARCTIC REGIONS; EARTH; EXPLORERS; NORTH POLE.)

PEAT In the picture below, peat is being cut from a peat bog. Peat is a kind of fuel. It is made from mosses and other plants that grow in bogs. When the plants die, they do not all rot away. The bog water has substances in it that keep them from

Peat is cut in squares and dried for fuel.

A COLLECTION OF PEBBLES

doing so. What is left of them remains in the bog. Little by little a thick layer of this half-rotted plant material may be formed. It can be dug up and dried. When it has been dried, it can be burned.

If the peat bogs of today should sink so that a great deal of mud was washed into them, the peat after thousands of years would turn into coal. All coal, scientists believe, was once peat.

Peat is not nearly as good a fuel as coal. A pound of peat gives much less heat than the same amount of coal gives. But people are glad to get peat if they cannot get coal.

The peat bogs of Ireland are famous. There are also peat bogs in Scotland and in a number of the countries of northern Europe. There are peat bogs in the United States, too, but America has so much coal that peat is not used as fuel. (See COAL; FUELS; IRELAND; MOSSES.)

PEBBLES Every pebble was once a part of a big mass of rock. In some way, it was broken off the big mass of rock. Perhaps a plant grew in a crack and broke the pebble off. Perhaps water froze in a crack. Perhaps the waves broke it off by hurling other pebbles against the rock. It might have been broken off in still some other way. There are a great many different kinds of pebbles because there are a great many different kinds of rock.

Pebbles are never smooth and round to begin with. But many of those we find in brooks and along the shore are. They have been rolled along by the water and rubbed against so many other pebbles that their rough edges have finally been worn away. Some pebbles are so worn that no one can tell what kind of rock they are made of without breaking them open.

In some places pebbles the shape of little doughnuts are found. They are sometimes called lucky stones. These pebbles are fossils. They are fossils of strange animals called sea lilies. (See EROSION; FOSSILS; MINERALS; QUARTZ; ROCKS.)

Porphyry

Quartz

Shale

Pumice

Diorite

Porphyry

Red Granite

Granite

Quartz

Quartz

Limestone

Quartzite

The emperor penguin may be over three feet tall.

PENGUINS The strange birds called penguins live along the shores of the southern oceans. Only one kind—the little Galapagos penguin—is found as far north as the equator. The islands where it lives are surrounded by a cold ocean current. Penguins feed on fish and other animals of the sea.

Some kinds of penguins are larger than others. The emperor penguin is perhaps the largest; it may be over three feet tall. This big penguin lives in the Far South. It can stand the darkness and cold of the long Antarctic winter.

All full-grown penguins are black and white. Except for size, they all look much alike as they waddle about. They can neither fly nor run. But those that live in regions of ice and snow can toboggan very well. And all penguins are good swimmers and divers. They use their wings as paddles.

Penguins nest in great colonies. They do not spend much time in nest-building. Some kinds lay their eggs on little mounds of stones. The emperor penguin lays its one egg on bare ice. To keep the egg from freezing, the mother bird rests it on her feet. Then she sits on the egg and keeps both the egg and her feet warm.

Baby penguins are fluffy and brown. For weeks they are fed by the father and mother birds. A young penguin does not take to the sea to get food for itself until it is about three months old. (See ANTARCTICA; BIRDS.)

PENICILLIN In 1928 Alexander Fleming, an English scientist, discovered a new drug. It was named penicillin. Penicillin was not used until ten years later. Now it is one of our biggest helps in fighting disease germs.

For several years after it first came into use this new drug was very scarce and very expensive. Today there is enough for everyone who needs it.

Penicillin comes from a kind of mold. The mold is very much like the common green mold that grows on bread and oranges and lemons.

After penicillin was discovered, scientists hunted for and found other drugs like it. A new name has been given to all the drugs that are like penicillin. They are called antibiotics. (See ANTIBIOTICS; MEDICINE; MOLDS.)

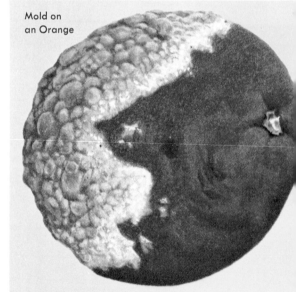

Mold on an Orange

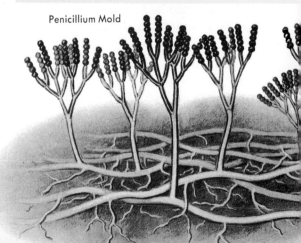

Penicillium Mold

PENINSULA A peninsula is an arm of land that reaches out into the sea. It is like a cape except that it is bigger. Since there is water almost all the way around it, a peninsula is almost an island. "Peninsula" comes from the Latin words meaning "nearly an island."

The southern continents have few peninsulas. But Europe, Asia, and North America have many. Many of the countries of Europe are on peninsulas. Among them are Norway, Sweden, Denmark, Spain, Portugal, Italy, and Greece. The Arabian Peninsula, the Malay Peninsula, India, and Korea are four of the peninsulas of Asia. And all Europe is really a huge peninsula of Asia. Among the peninsulas of North America are Alaska, Lower California, the Florida Peninsula, and Yucatán.

PENN, WILLIAM (1644-1718) The city hall in Philadelphia is sometimes called the "biggest penholder in the world." For at the top of this building there is an enormous statue of William Penn. It is 37 feet tall.

William Penn is honored in this way because he founded Philadelphia. In fact, he founded the whole state of Pennsylvania. He sent a band of Quakers, or Friends, to America in 1681, and arrived himself in 1682. His statue in Philadelphia shows him in the broadbrimmed hat and the wide-skirted coat the Quakers wore.

The son of a wealthy English admiral, William Penn studied in famous Oxford University. But he was expelled because of his ideas about religion. Not long afterward he became a Quaker. The Quakers at that time were despised in England. Their religion was too different from the religion of most of the English.

Penn was soon the leading Quaker in England. The king of England owed Penn's father a great deal of money. To pay his debt, the king gave William Penn, after his father's death, thousands of acres of land in America. Penn set about founding a colony on this land. In the New World the Quakers would be able to worship as they chose. The new colony was named Pennsylvania. This name means "Penn's woods."

The nickname of Philadelphia tells a great deal about the Quakers who founded it. Its nickname is "City of Brotherly Love." William Penn let the people make their own laws and rule themselves. The Quakers treated one another well. They treated the Indians round about well, too. The people of Pennsylvania were at peace with the Indians when many of the other colonies were fighting with them.

Penn loved the colony he had founded, but he did not spend much of his life in it. Business forced him to live mostly in England. Even so, he is the most famous of the founders of the 13 colonies. (See COLONIAL LIFE IN AMERICA; PENNSYLVANIA; PHILADELPHIA; QUAKERS.)

William Penn treated the Indians fairly.

PENNSYLVANIA This Middle Atlantic state has no seacoast on the Atlantic. But by way of Delaware Bay and the Delaware River large ocean vessels can reach Philadelphia. Pennsylvania is in the heart of the Appalachian Region, a region of mountains and plateaus. A small area in the southeast is coastal plain and another small section in the northwest is lake plain. "Pennsylvania" means "Penn's Woods." It honors the father of William Penn, the founder of the colony of Pennsylvania. Pennsylvania was nicknamed the "Keystone State" because six of the original thirteen states are to the north and east of it and six are to the south.

The earliest white settlers in the Pennsylvania country were Dutch, Swedes, and Finns. They came in the early 1600's. A group of Quakers, sent by William Penn, arrived in 1681. Penn himself came a year later. Penn made friends with the Indians and treated them well. Among the later settlers in the colony were Germans, Welsh, Scots, and Scotch-Irish.

In the fertile valleys of Pennsylvania, the colonial farmers produced many food products. Townspeople started little industries that today are outstanding. In Penn's city of Philadelphia they made woolen goods, hats, iron, and glass. Nearby, on the Delaware River, they built ships for coastal and ocean trade.

In 1787 Pennsylvania entered the Union as the second state—next after Delaware. The state capital is now at Harrisburg. Pennsylvania is not a large state, but it ranks third in population. Only New York and California have more people. Seven out of ten Pennsylvanians live in cities. Pennsylvania is one of the leading industrial states in the country. It ranks next to New York in value of its factory products.

Although only a small number of Pennsylvanians are farmers, the farms are fine. On them are produced many crops needed for the food of the nearby cities: dairy products, livestock, vegetables, and fruits.

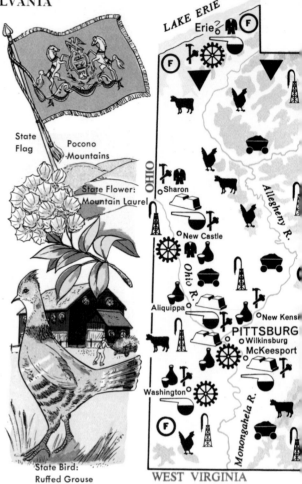

State Flag

Pocono Mountains

State Flower: Mountain Laurel

State Bird: Ruffed Grouse

The first oil well in the United States was drilled near Titusville in 1859. Today there are still some producing oil and natural gas wells, but coal is the most valuable mineral. Pennsylvania produces almost all the hard coal mined in the United States. The vast amounts of soft coal furnish fuel for the big manufacturing industries in the region.

Pennsylvania ranks first in the making of iron and steel, locomotives, and steel railway cars. Pittsburgh is one of the chief iron and steel manufacturing centers of the world. Its position where the Allegheny and Monongahela Rivers join to make the Ohio River has helped its growth. A very large new steel mill has been built on the Delaware River not far from Philadelphia. Iron ore from foreign countries can be brought by ship to this plant. A new town, Fairless Hills, has grown up around it.

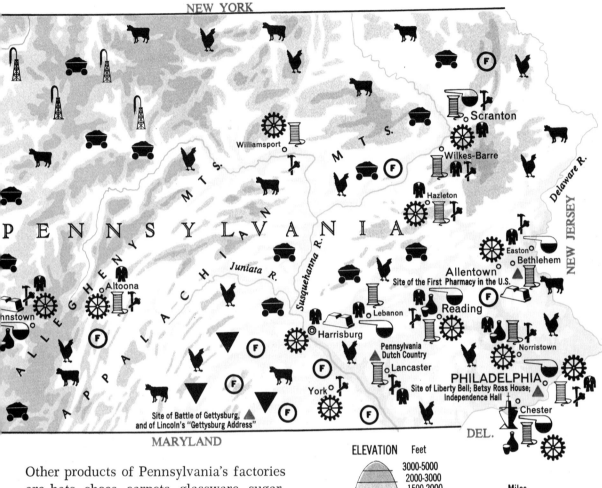

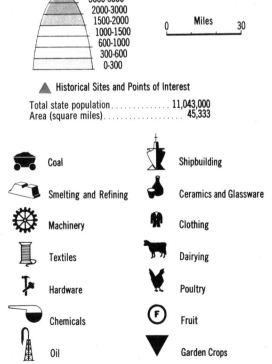

ELEVATION   Feet

3000-5000
2000-3000
1500-2000
1000-1500
600-1000
300-600
0-300

Miles
0   30

▲ Historical Sites and Points of Interest

Total state population.............. 11,043,000
Area (square miles)................... 45,333

Coal

Smelting and Refining

Machinery

Textiles

Hardware

Chemicals

Oil

Shipbuilding

Ceramics and Glassware

Clothing

Dairying

Poultry

(F) Fruit

▼ Garden Crops

Other products of Pennsylvania's factories are hats, shoes, carpets, glassware, sugar, chemicals, and candy.

Among the many things Pennsylvanians take pride in are their beautiful woodlands. Although most of the forest trees in "Penn's Woods" were cut down to make room for homes, farms, cities, and roads, there are again vast areas of lovely trees. Much credit is due to the work of a Pennsylvania governor, Gifford Pinchot (PIN sho). He was one of the first to work for the conservation of America's forests.

Drums called soldiers to battle.

PERCUSSION INSTRUMENTS The musical instruments in the pictures on this page are percussion instruments. They make their sounds when they are shaken or struck. There are other percussion instruments besides those that are pictured. Among them are the kettledrum, the bass drum, and the marimba. Many percussion instruments are found in a symphony orchestra. Drums and cymbals are found in marching bands, marimbas in marimba bands and sometimes in regular orchestras.

Some percussion instruments give off a number of definite musical tones. Among them are the kettledrums, bells, celesta, chimes, xylophone, and marimba. Thirty-seven notes, for instance, can be played on some sets of orchestral bells. The notes go from middle C to the C above high C.

The bass drum, snare drum, cymbals, tambourine, castanets, triangle, and gong are not usually played for the notes they make. They are used to accent the rhythm, to make the music louder, or to give a special kind of sound that is needed. Tambourines give a light, tinkling sound. A sharper tinkling sound comes from a triangle. Castanets give a pleasant click. A snare drum produces a rattle; cymbals and gongs a metallic crash. "Boom" is the best word for the sound of a bass drum.

In every musical instrument something moves back and forth very fast to make the sound. We say that it vibrates. In the bells, chimes, cymbals, gong, celesta, and triangle the vibrating parts are made of metal. In all the kinds of drums the vibrating parts are made of tightly stretched skin, or parchment. In castanets, marim-

Cymbals and triangles help accent music.

bas, and xylophones the vibrating parts are wood. Wood, metal, and skin give off quite different sounds.

An instrument may give off one kind of sound when struck with one kind of stick or hammer and a quite different sound when struck with another kind. A kettledrum player has two or three sets of drumsticks. He usually uses drumsticks with balls at the end that are covered with lamb's wool or felt. For very loud sounds he uses drumsticks that have heads covered with leather and drumsticks with wooden heads for a sharper sound.

Kettledrums are the most important percussion instruments in a symphony orches-

Castanets and tambourines are used in dancing.

tra. A kettledrum player must have a very good ear for pitch. As the key changes in a composition the orchestra is playing, the kettledrum player must change the pitch of his drums very quickly. He does so by tightening or loosening the screws that hold the calfskin head in place. The tighter the skin, the higher the tone the kettledrum gives off.

The marimba is a rather new instrument in the United States. It came from Africa by way of Latin America. A marimba is much like a xylophone. Under each wooden slab there is a sound box. At the bottom of each box there is a hole with a piece of thin skin stretched over it. The skin makes a peculiar buzzing sound when the player strikes a slab. There are small marimbas and large marimbas. Large marimbas are often played by several players.

Steel marimbas, or marimbaphones, are now being made in the United States. (See BAND; BELLS; DRUMS; ORCHESTRA; SOUND; STRINGED INSTRUMENTS; WIND INSTRUMENTS; XYLOPHONE.)

PERFUMES Roses, lilies-of-the-valley, violets, and many other flowers are very fragrant. Their sweet smell comes from a special oil in them. This oil attracts the insects that are needed to carry pollen from flower to flower.

The fragrance of flowers is so pleasant that it is no wonder people got the idea of making perfume. What they had to learn to do was to take the fragrant oil from the flowers and add to it something to make the fragrance last. They found that certain materials from animals help perfume keep its odor. One is ambergris, a waxy substance from whales. Others come from the musk-deer, beaver, and civet cat. Alcohol, too, is used in perfumes.

There are other sweet-smelling plant oils besides those in flowers. They are found in the leaves, stems, roots, fruits, or even seeds of various plants. These oils are often added to flower oils.

Orange Blossoms

It takes a great many flowers to make a little perfume. It takes, for instance, a ton of rose petals to make a pound of rose oil, or attar of roses. But much of the perfume of today does not come from flowers. Strange as it seems, much of it comes from coal tar. Scientists have learned to make from coal tar perfumes that smell like those from flowers. They are also able to make from it new fragrances.

Perfumes have been made for thousands of years. Perfume jars have been found in the tombs of ancient Egypt. The ancient Romans, too, used much perfume. In the days of Columbus the ships that brought spices from the East brought perfumes, too. Perfumes are still popular today. Many millions of dollars' worth are sold every year. (See AMBERGRIS; BULGARIA; COAL TAR; POLLINATION.)

Violets and sweet peas are often used in the making of perfumes.

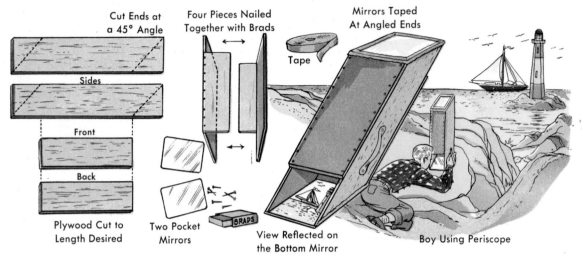

Cut Ends at a 45° Angle

Four Pieces Nailed Together with Brads

Mirrors Taped At Angled Ends

Tape

Sides

Front

Back

Plywood Cut to Length Desired

Two Pocket Mirrors

BRADS

View Reflected on the Bottom Mirror

Boy Using Periscope

HOMEMADE PERISCOPE

PERISCOPE The word "periscope" means "see around." With a periscope it is possible to see around corners. With a periscope it is possible, too, to see over walls and other such obstacles. Often some of the people in a crowd watching a parade have periscopes so that they can see over the heads of the people in front. A periscope is an important part of a submarine. A submarine's periscope makes it possible for the crew to see above the surface of the water when the submarine is submerged.

The simplest kind of periscope is a tube with an opening near each end and two slanting mirrors inside the tube, one facing each opening. The mirrors must slant in just the right way so that light which strikes one mirror is reflected down the tube to the other mirror and then to the eyes of the person using the periscope.

The periscopes of submarines are much more complicated. They have prisms to reflect the light and lenses to make ships that are far away show clearly. The tubes of these periscopes can be made longer or shorter. The crew of a submarine 44 feet under water can still see what is going on above the surface.

It is easy to build a simple periscope. The important thing is to have the mirrors at the right angle. (See LENSES; LIGHT; MIRRORS; SUBMARINES.)

PERPETUAL MOTION For centuries people have dreamed of making a perpetual motion machine—one that, once started, would keep on running all by itself forever. Fortunes have been spent in trying to build such a machine. But no one has ever been able to build one, and scientists tell us that no one ever will be able to do so.

A perpetual motion machine is impossible because in every machine there is some friction. Little by little a machine slows down unless more energy is provided. A perpetual motion machine would have to furnish its own energy, and this is something that no machine can do.

Some musicians have been interested in the idea of motion that goes on forever. There are several compositions called "Perpetual Motion." (See ENERGY; FRICTION; PHYSICS.)

PERSIA In 547 B.C. Cyrus II, the ruler of the young country of Persia, marched against Croesus, the king of Lydia. Lydia was a strong nation in the part of the world we now call Asia Minor. King Croesus was famous for his gold. Many other rulers of the time longed to be as rich as he was. Croesus sent out his troops to meet Cyrus. In the battle neither side won.

Winter was coming on, and Croesus thought that Cyrus would take his armies back to Persia to wait for better weather. He himself took his troops back to his capital, Sardis. But Cyrus had no idea of turning back. With his baggage camels in the front of his army, he pushed ahead. Croesus then sent his fine mounted horsemen to meet Cyrus' troops. But when the horses saw the strange-looking camels they would not go toward them. Probably the smell of the camels as well as the sight of them terrified the horses. Cyrus won the battle easily. He captured Croesus and soon conquered all of Lydia. The gold he won from Croesus helped him go on to conquer all of western Asia and build up the biggest empire the world had ever seen.

The story of the Persians begins four or five hundred years before the time of Cyrus. Then tribes from eastern Europe moved down into the great plateau which we now call the plateau of Iran. Their fighters came riding horseback. Chariots drawn by horses had been used by the Assyrians and the Egyptians, but soldiers on horseback were new. These newcomers spread over the plateau. Some moved eastward toward India. Some moved westward to the borders of Babylonia and Assyria. Some of those that settled near Babylonia became the Medes. Others moved into a region called Parsa and became the Per-

Carving of Darius and Eight Conquered Kings

sians. The Medes built up a strong kingdom before the Persians did.

Most early empires grew slowly. But not Persia. It grew in one man's rather short lifetime—the lifetime of Cyrus II—from a small kingdom into a great empire.

Cyrus was a new kind of conqueror. He did not force the ways of the Persians on the peoples he conquered. He let them keep their own customs and their own religions. In most cases he treated their rulers well.

Although Cyrus founded a great empire, it was not as large as he had hoped. He wanted to add Egypt to it. But he was killed in battle before he could do so.

Cambyses, the son of Cyrus, carried out his father's plan of conquering Egypt. But while he was in Egypt revolts began in his empire in Asia. He hurried home, but died

Persia About 500 B.C.
Present Day Nations and Boundaries are Shown

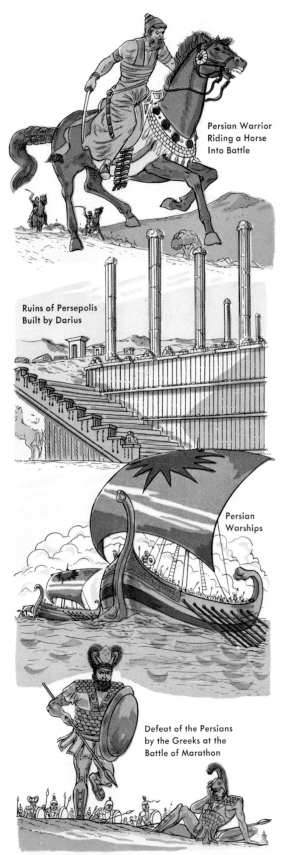

Persian Warrior
Riding a Horse
Into Battle

Ruins of Persepolis
Built by Darius

Persian
Warships

Defeat of the Persians
by the Greeks at the
Battle of Marathon

before he could put down the revolts. Darius, a nobleman, became the next king.

Darius saw that under Cyrus the empire had been too loosely held together. After fighting down all the revolts—in 19 battles he defeated nine kings—he divided his empire up into "satraps" and put a Persian in charge of each one. He built roads so that his armies could be sent quickly to any place where there was trouble. For himself he built great royal palaces, first at Susa and then at Persepolis.

On the walls of his palaces Darius had artists carve the figures of his "Ten Thousand Immortals." They were soldiers who had fought with him for the glory of Persia.

Even though his empire was even larger than the empire of Cyrus, Darius set out to make it larger still. He marched his armies into Europe and conquered the region north of Greece. Then he decided to take Greece itself. Here he made a mistake. In 490 B.C. his army was very badly defeated by the Greeks in the Battle of Marathon. A revolt in Egypt forced him to give up any idea of trying again to take Greece. He died soon afterward.

For fear he would be forgotten, Darius had his picture carved on the wall of a mountain. Along with his own figure, he included the figures of ten kings he had conquered. He also had stories of his exploits carved in the stone. They are written in three languages: ancient Persian, Babylonian, and Elamite. Carvings on his tomb tell about the great power of Darius too. One of the inscriptions says, "I am Darius, the Great King, King of Kings, King of countries containing all kinds of men, King in this great earth far and wide . . . a Persian, son of a Persian. . . ."

Xerxes, the son of Darius, became king when his father died. Xerxes did not like fighting. He liked building palaces and monuments much better. But he felt bound to try to avenge the defeat his father had suffered at the hands of Greece. But he, too, was defeated. As he sat on a throne

16th Century Miniature Painting

Courtesy of Metropolitan Museum of Art—
Gift of Alexander Smith Cochran, 1913

Donald L. Ferguson-Monkmeyer

The Mosque at
Isfahan, Iran

**OUTSTANDING
EXAMPLES OF
PERSIAN ART**

Manuscript
Painting

Courtesy of Metropolitan Museum of Art—Rogers Fund, 1913

on the seashore, he watched the Greek ships destroy his fleet in a great naval battle, the Battle of Salamis. Xerxes was bitter about his defeat. He never again left his capitals of Persepolis and Susa.

Four weak rulers followed Xerxes. The empire began to break up. It was not hard, in 331 B.C., for Alexander the Great of Macedon to defeat the Persian king and add Persia to his empire.

The Persians borrowed many of their ideas from the ancient peoples they conquered. They borrowed cuneiform writing —writing with wedge-shaped strokes on clay or brick tablets—from the Babylonians. From the Arameans they learned to write in ink on papyrus. From the Babylonians they learned to build walls of sun-dried brick. From the Egyptians they learned to make stone doorways and pillars. In art they combined ideas of both the west and the east with their own.

From the Lydians they got the idea of coining gold and silver. Their money was a great help to trade. From the Phoenicians they learned to build boats. Persian sailors sailed over the Mediterranean and even out into the Atlantic. Before the days of

the Persians most trade was in silver and gold and other luxuries. Much of the Persians' trade was in common things such as clothing and household goods.

The Persians tried to make life better for their people by irrigating dry lands, by draining swamps, and by improving agriculture. They brought in new fruits and crop plants from other lands.

In the great days of Persia a new religion arose there. It was based on the teachings of Zoroaster (zo ro AS ter). Zoroaster taught that to be good a person must think good thoughts, say kind words, and do good deeds. He must be kind to animals. A just ruler must defend his people, feed the poor, and protect the weak.

Although they were conquered, the Persians were not destroyed. Now they rule themselves. The country's modern name is Iran. (See CROESUS; IRAN; NEAR EAST.)

Andes Mountains

Raising Cotton

Peruvian Flag

Llama

Indian

ECUADOR

COLOMBIA

Amazon R.

Iquitos

Piura

Marañón R.

Chiclayo

Trujillo

Chimbote

Pucallpa

Ucayali R.

BRAZIL

Cerro de Pasco
La Oroya

Callao LIMA

Huancayo
Ayacucho

Cuzco

BOLIVIA

Lake Titicaca

Puno

Arequipa

Mollendo

PACIFIC OCEAN

CHILE

Total population.......... 9,651,000
Area (square miles)........ 482,258

Cotton

Sugar

Oil

Copper

Sheep

MILES
0   200

ELEVATION Feet

Over 10000
5000- 10000
2000- 5000
1000- 2000
0- 1000

PERU This country of South America is a little more than three times as big as California. The Andes Mountains run north and south through it. They divide the country into three parts. There is the mountainous region itself. In it are high, sunny mountain valleys and peaks more than 20,000 feet high. Then there is a low, narrow desert region between the mountains and the Pacific Ocean. And on the other side of the mountainous land, there is a hot, wet lowland region.

Until recent years, no place in the highland could be reached by train or car from either lowland. All travel from one region to another was hard. Even today, the people of the different regions are much shut off from one another.

Most people of the mountains are Indian or part Indian. There was a great Indian empire in South America when Columbus came to the New World. The Indians were Incas. The capital of their empire was Cuzco, now a city of Peru. It is high in the mountains. But days are warmer there than one might think. The city is only half as far from the equator as the southern tip of Florida is. And it gets a great many hours of sunshine.

Today, Indians in the highlands live very much as their Inca ancestors did. Indian farmers raise wheat, barley, potatoes, and some "dwarf" corn. Some of their farms are about as high as Pikes Peak and are said to be the highest farms in the world. Shepherds tend flocks of sheep, alpacas, and vicuñas on mountainside pastures that are even higher. Some of the shepherd huts may be the very highest homes in the world. Other Indians work in mines. Not only silver and gold, as in Inca days, but also copper and the rare metal vanadium are now mined in Peru.

Planes now fly between Cuzco and Lima, Peru's capital. In Cuzco, tourists see Inca ruins. In a cathedral built after Inca times, they can see a silver altar and a dragon carved from one big emerald.

Lima is Peru's largest city. It is in the desert lowland. Lima was founded by Spaniards more than 400 years ago. It has its old Spanish look still, and the oldest university in the New World. But it has modern streets and buildings, too. Many people go to its famous beaches on summer days, when the shops and offices close at two o'clock. Ocean breezes make the climate pleasanter than one would expect.

A river that flows through the city is one of more than 50 rivers that cross the strip of lowland desert. Weather is warm the year round, and land along the rivers is fertile. On land near enough to the streams to be irrigated, farmers raise wonderful crops of many kinds. Cotton and sugar are exported. So is petroleum, which comes from wells in the lowland. Farmers keep the soil rich by using guano. Guano is bird manure. There are great stores of it on islands near the coast. Many thousands of seabirds nest on those islands. Most people in the desert strip are part Spanish and part Indian.

Most of the few Indians who live in the hot, wet east lowland make a living by selling mahogany and other forest products. Perhaps this area is a "land of the future." (See ANDES; INCAS.)

PETRIFIED WOOD The logs in the pictures below are petrified; they have been made over into stone. The trees they came from died millions of years ago.

The story of every piece of petrified wood is very much like this: A tree fell to the ground. It was soon covered up, perhaps with mud, perhaps with lava and ashes from a volcano. Instead of rotting, it was gradually changed by the water in the ground. This water had minerals in it. As the tree lay buried, the water took away the wood, one tiny particle at a time, and left a tiny mineral particle in place of each particle of wood. After many centuries the wood itself was all gone and there was a piece of solid stone in its place.

Petrified wood shows much of the pattern of the wood it was made from. Scientists can tell a great deal about the trees of long ago by studying petrified wood.

Much petrified wood is beautiful in color. Some is so beautiful that it is used in jewelry. The minerals give it its color.

A petrified log may be four feet across and 100 feet long. Of course most logs are not so large. In some places they lie on top of the ground because the material that covered them up has been washed away. An area where there are many petrified logs is called a petrified forest. There are several petrified forests in the United States. (See GEOLOGY.)

A Fallen Tree in the Petrified Forest

Petrified Log

Petrified Stump

Sea Life of Long Ago

PETROLEUM "They've struck oil" is exciting news, and good news, too. It was not always good news. In the early days of the United States one way of getting salt was to dig wells to reach salt water deep underground. A man digging for salt was very much disappointed if he found oil instead. Now anyone who digs for oil and gets salt water feels he has lost a fortune.

The oil that men dig for is petroleum. Its name comes from Latin words meaning "rock oil." When it first comes out of the earth, the rock oil, or crude oil, is a thick, dark liquid.

Scientists think that petroleum came from the bodies of very tiny plants and animals that lived in the shallow seas of millions of years ago. These plants and animals fell to the bottom of the water when they died and were buried in mud there. In time this mud was covered by layers of sand and by layers made up mostly of the shells of little sea animals and by more layers of mud. Gradually oil was produced from the buried plants and animals, but no one is exactly sure how. There are different ideas about it.

As millions of years went by, the layers of sand and shells and mud that had settled to the floor of the sea became solid rock. The mud became shale, the sand became sandstone, and the shells became limestone. Sandstone and limestone have tiny holes, or pores, in them. Shale has pores,

too, but they are even smaller. Most of the oil collected in the pores of the sandstone and limestone. These rocks were so porous that the oil could travel from place to place in them. It collected in various areas where the rocks were wrinkled up to form traps for it. Oil is lighter than water and can be held up in a rock trap by water below it.

Petroleum has been known for many, many centuries. As a rule it is deep in the ground, but in places it seeps up through cracks to the surface. Ancient peoples found this surface petroleum and used it for medicine and for fuel for their fires. They used the asphalt sometimes left when the rest evaporated for holding brick together in floors and walls and for making boats waterproof. But for a long, long time no one thought of digging for oil.

We know now that petroleum is a mixture of a great many materials. It can be separated into the many different compounds in it. Among them are gasoline, kerosene, motor oil, grease, petroleum jelly, paraffin, and asphalt. Separating petroleum into its parts is called refining it.

One reason people were so slow about hunting for oil was that for a long time they could get all the oil and grease they needed from plants and animals. But about 100 years ago the picture changed. The machine age had begun. Better kinds of oil and grease were needed to keep the machines running smoothly. Kerosene was needed, too, for kerosene had been found to be useful in lamps.

The first oil well in the United States was drilled in 1859. It was drilled in Titusville, Pa., by Colonel Edwin L. Drake. Oil was reached 69½ feet below the surface of the ground. The well yielded 25 barrels of oil a day. Other wells soon followed.

At this time the automobile and airplane had not been invented. No one was interested in gasoline. It was thrown away. Millions of gallons of gasoline were wasted before automobiles and airplanes appeared and began using it in enormous amounts.

It is no easy task to separate petroleum into the different substances in it. The general plan is this: The petroleum is heated until most of it changes to a vapor. The vapor goes to a tall tower. The lightest goes to the top of the tower, the heaviest to the bottom. The vapor is drawn off at various heights in the tower. It is changed back to liquid form. The lightest vapor becomes the lightest liquid—gasoline. The next-lightest vapor becomes the next-lightest liquid—kerosene—and so on.

The world today uses several billion barrels of oil every year. From it come not only gasoline, kerosene, various oils and greases, but hundreds of other products. Among them are drugs, dyes, and plastics.

Among the countries where there are great oil fields are the United States, Venezuela, the U.S.S.R., Saudi Arabia, Kuwait, Iran, and Iraq. A constant hunt for oil is going on. Oil companies hire geologists (scientists who study rocks) to look for places where oil is likely to be trapped. But geologists can never be sure. The only sure way to find out is to drill down and see.

Drilling for oil means first building a derrick. This derrick holds long sections of drill pipe in place. At the bottom of one piece of drill pipe there is a bit with large cutting teeth. An engine whirls it around

Early Oil Derricks

and it cuts its way down into the ground, taking the pipe with it. New sections of pipe are added as they are needed. At last it may reach a layer where there is oil. Perhaps there is natural gas in the rock trap along with the oil. If so, it may push the oil up through the pipe. It may even shoot it high into the air. But as a rule pumps must be used to raise the oil.

Some wells go very deep. The record for drilling is more than four miles. A deep well may cost over a million dollars.

A well may be a failure even when one close by is very good. There are fortunes to be won—or they can be lost—in hunting for petroleum. (See ASPHALT; FUELS; GEOLOGY; NATURAL GAS.)

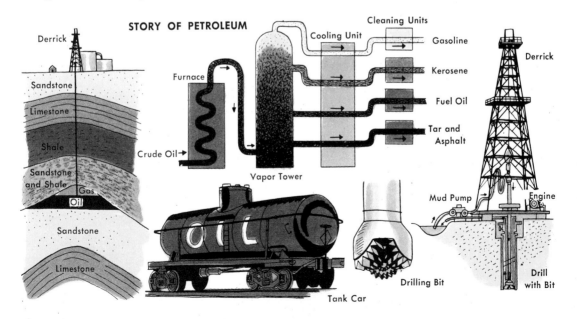

STORY OF PETROLEUM

Derrick

Sandstone

Limestone

Shale

Sandstone and Shale

Gas

Oil

Sandstone

Limestone

Furnace

Crude Oil

Vapor Tower

Cooling Unit

Cleaning Units

Gasoline

Kerosene

Fuel Oil

Tar and Asphalt

Derrick

Mud Pump

Engine

Drill with Bit

Drilling Bit

Tank Car

The soft, furry rabbit makes a gentle and friendly pet.

PETS Any animal that is kept for the fun of having it around is a pet. The commonest pets are cats and dogs. But there are dozens of other animals that make good pets. The pictures show some of them. Here are some others: lamb, kid, tropical fish, hamster, skunk, chameleon, and parakeet.

A pet should be chosen with great care. Some of the pets in the pictures most of us would not want at all. A person who wants a pet must not think just of himself. He must think of the people around him. A mischievous or noisy pet can be a great nuisance to neighbors.

A person choosing a pet must think of the comfort of the animal, too. No pet can be comfortable unless it has plenty of the right kind of food and a clean place to stay. Koalas are like live teddy bears with their soft fur and cuddly look. But they have to have a special kind of eucalyptus leaves to eat. In choosing a pet, then, these are good questions to think about:

Will the right food be hard to get?

Does the animal need a special kind of cage or pen?

Will the animal be a nuisance because it makes too much noise?

Is the animal the right size for the home in which it will live?

Will the animal need more exercise than it can be given?

Is the animal easy to keep clean?

Will it be likely to hurt someone?

Most people seem to want a playful pet. Cats and dogs are the best choices. Tropical fish are interesting to raise and care for, but they do not play.

If a person decides he wants a dog or a cat, there are many kinds to select from. As a rule, short-haired dogs are best for cities. Beagles, Boston terriers, and dachshunds make good city pets. Great Danes are short-haired, but they are big for city living. It is hard in a city to give them all the exercise they need. They need a great deal of food, too. There are other big short-haired dogs that are better for towns or the country than for a crowded city. Cockers and Scotties are long-haired. They are better off away from crowded, dirty streets. Setters, springers, and collies are especially good as country dogs.

No house cats are too big for city homes. But the short-haired cats are much easier to take care of than the long-haired ones.

Fashions change in pets. Parakeets are now more popular than parrots. Pug dogs were once very common, but now there are not very many of them.

Pets are often bothered by such pests as fleas, ticks, and lice. Taking good care of a pet means keeping it free of such pests. Pets have diseases, too. There are animal

Ornamental Cock

Burro

Cheetah

Pigeon

Peacock

Fighting Cocks

Squirrel

Crow

Monkey

Parrot

Canary

Samoyed

Angora Cat

Spaniel

Siamese Cat

Jerboa

Goldfish

Turtle

Rabbits

Singing Cricket

Guinea Pig

Dancing Bear

doctors that can help them if they get sick. These doctors are called veterinarians. There are animal hospitals, too. A sick pet can get good care in one of these special hospitals. (See ANIMAL BREEDING; CATS; DOGS; DOMESTICATED ANIMALS; PARASITES; TROPICAL FISHES; VETERINARY MEDICINE.)

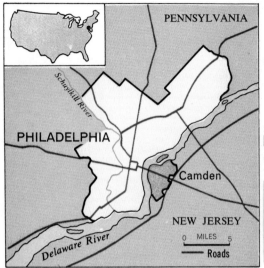

PHILADELPHIA Many cities have nicknames. Philadelphia has a very pleasant one—"The City of Brotherly Love." The name Philadelphia comes from the Greek words meaning "brotherly love."

Philadelphia is in Pennsylvania where the Schuylkill (SKOOL kil) River flows into the big Delaware River. The city is 90 miles from the Atlantic, but big ocean vessels can reach it.

The story of the city begins in 1681. It was founded by William Penn, the Quaker to whom the king of England gave all of Pennsylvania. William Penn's statue on top of the city hall now overlooks the recently built Penn Center.

In the early history of the United States Philadelphia played a very important part. Some of the greatest American patriots lived there; Benjamin Franklin was one of them. In 1774 the First Continental Congress was held there. The next year the Second Continental Congress was held there. The Declaration of Independence was signed there. It was signed in Independence Hall. After the colonies won their freedom, the convention that agreed on the Constitution for the new country met there. For many years (1683 to 1799) Philadelphia was the capital of Pennsylvania. For 10 years (1790 to 1800) it was the capital of the United States.

There are a number of "firsts" in Philadelphia's story. The first newspaper in the Middle Colonies was printed there. So was the first daily newspaper in the whole country. The country's first hospital was built there. And the city was the home of the country's first art center.

Philadelphia is the fourth-largest city in the United States today. Only New York City, Chicago, and Los Angeles are larger. It is a great port city. Railroads meet ocean-going boats there. The freight yards and docks give work to thousands of people. Thousands more are employed in works where stainless steel trains are made, in a government navy yard, and in publishing houses. A great many people are needed in factories, among them factories where carpets and rugs are made.

The city has a number of skyscrapers. Some are office buildings; others are banks, stores, or hotels. There are many schools and colleges. The University of Pennsylvania and Temple are two of the most famous. Independence Hall now faces a beautiful new mall, or parkway, on one side and the new National Historical Park on another. Philadelphia, with its mixture of old and new, is well worth visiting. (See DECLARATION OF INDEPENDENCE; FRANKLIN, BENJAMIN; PATRIOTS; PENN, WILLIAM; PENNSYLVANIA.)

PHILIPPINES, REPUBLIC OF THE

On the first round-the-world voyage ever made, Magellan and a band of Spanish sailors, in 1521, discovered the Philippine Islands. They lie off the southeast coast of Asia, in the Pacific Ocean. Later Spanish explorers named the islands the Philippines, in honor of King Philip II of Spain. The lively, bright people living on the islands they called Filipinos.

For 300 years the Philippines were part of the Spanish Empire. In 1898, as a result of the Spanish-American War, they became a possession of the United States. The American government helped the Filipinos to improve health conditions and to build good highways and schools. On July 4, 1946, the Philippines became an independent country. Quezon City is the new capital. Most of the government offices are still in Manila, the old capital.

There are more than 7,000 islands in the Philippines. Most of them are unnamed bare rocks, too small to have any people living on them. Eleven islands make up almost the whole country. Most of the people live on the two largest islands—Luzon and Mindanao. Filipinos travel largely by boat and by airplane.

Most Filipinos are farmers. Hills and mountains cover much of the islands. But there is enough lowland to let the Filipinos raise all the food their 21,000,000 people need and to have some products to ship to other lands. The climate is tropical, with heavy rains. Rice and corn are the main food crops. Sugar, copra from coconuts and abaca are the chief products exported. Abaca is a fiber used in ropemaking. It is often called Manila hemp. The abaca plant which yields this fiber looks somewhat like a banana plant.

Most Filipinos work on small farms with some help from the water buffalo. Much of the work is done by hand. Filipinos raise few animals. Their meat is mostly fish.

Some Filipinos are miners. They dig gold, iron, chromium, and other ores. Others do lumbering. Heavy forests cover much of the land of the islands.

The Philippines have only one great city. It is Manila, with about 1,000,000 people. Most of the country's factories are in Manila. It is the chief seaport. It is a center for airlines that link the Philippines with the outside world.

Total population 22,056,100
Area (square miles) 114,830

Philippine women make many things by hand

Phoenicians sailed the Mediterranean Sea 5,000 years ago, trading with countries along the shores.

PHOENICIANS About 5,000 years ago some desert nomads settled along the eastern end of the Mediterranean Sea. In time, since other peoples pushed into the region, the descendants of these nomads had left to them only a narrow strip of coastland about 200 miles long. It is not surprising that they turned to the sea. They had small fishing boats. Now they built bigger ones. Before long they were roaming the seas as their ancestors had once roamed the desert. They began trading with other countries on the shores of the Mediterranean. The Greeks called these people Phoenicians. The name "Phoenician" came, it is thought, from a Greek word for red.

One of the things the Phoenicians had to trade was a beautiful red dye. They made it from a shellfish found on their seacoast. Although the dye was red, it came to be called Tyrian purple. It cost so much that only kings and very rich people could buy it. The idea that purple is a royal color came from the use of this dye.

The Phoenicians grew to be better and better sailors. They built better and better boats. Their biggest boats were 70 feet long. They had both sails and oars. In these boats the Phoenicians sailed from one end of the Mediterranean to the other. They even went out into the Atlantic and sailed all the way to the British Isles to get

tin. On the north coast of Africa, far away from their homeland, they founded the city of Carthage. Carthage became the rival of the great city of Rome.

As the Phoenicians learned to be better sailors they also learned to be better traders. They traded in things they made themselves. They also traded in things made in other lands. Some of their wares were wonderful. They sold beautiful cloth made of linen and wool. They sold jewels, and things made of silver and gold. They sold perfumes and spices.

Three large ports had grown up on their coast. They were Tyre and Sidon and Biblos. Tyre was famous for its Tyrian purple. This city was built on islands a short distance from the shore. One of the first aqueducts built anywhere in the world was built to bring water to this city. Sidon was famous for its glass. Biblos traded in papyrus. Papyrus was used for books before paper was invented. The Greek word for books came from the name of this city. So did our word "Bible."

The Phoenicians did not have any new ideas about government or science or art. They did not write any great books, or even any books at all. They were simple sailors and traders. But in one way they helped civilization a very great deal. In their journeys to carry on trading they carried the alphabet to the Greeks. For this reason the Phoenicians are sometimes called the missionaries of civilization.

The Phoenicians were not strong enough to hold their own against their larger neighbors. They came under the rule of first one and then another. At last, about 2,000 years ago they became a part of the great Roman Empire. From then on they were lost as a separate people. (See ALPHABET; DYES; TRADE.)

PHONOGRAPH The word "phonograph" comes from two Greek words. They mean "sound" and "write." A phonograph plays records on which sounds are "written down," or recorded. Music on records is sometimes called "canned music." To understand a phonograph one has to know that sound is caused by vibration. "Vibration" means rapid moving back and forth.

Edison invented the phonograph. To make a record he took a short tube, or cylinder, and wrapped it in tin foil. With a motor he made the tube turn around and around. A needle touched the record. This needle was fastened to a thin sheet of metal called a diaphragm. When sound waves struck this diaphragm they made it vibrate. The vibrations of the diaphragm made the needle vibrate and made a faint wavy groove in the tin foil.

Playing a record was just the opposite of making one. The record was put on the phonograph. It was made to turn around and around. A needle fastened to a diaphragm rested in the groove. As the point of the needle traveled along the groove, the waves in the groove made the needle vibrate. The vibrating needle made the diaphragm vibrate, and the diaphragm produced again the sounds that had made the needle vibrate in the beginning.

In making records today the needle is not fastened to the diaphragm. An electric current carries the vibrations from the diaphragm to the needle. In the phonograph that plays the record, an electric current often carries the vibrations from the needle to the diaphragm. Modern records are flat, not tube-shaped.

Today phonographs are often called record players. Many record players have four different speeds. When a person buys a record he should know at what speed it is to be played. Perhaps it must turn around 78 times a minute. Perhaps instead it must turn 16, 33⅓, or 45 times a minute. He must know that his record player can turn the record at the right speed.

There are many other ways in which records and record players have been improved. There are now automatic record changers, tape records, hi-fi (high fidelity) records and record players, and stereophonic sound set-ups. How different they all are from their simple beginnings! (See EDISON, THOMAS ALVA; SOUND.)

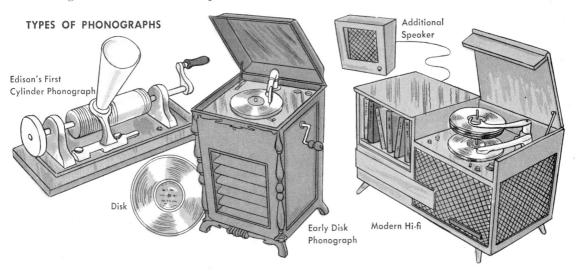

TYPES OF PHONOGRAPHS

Edison's First Cylinder Phonograph

Disk

Additional Speaker

Early Disk Phonograph

Modern Hi-fi

Phosphorus helps make matches catch fire.

PHOSPHORUS Some materials that will burn can be set on fire much more easily than others. Phosphorus is one of those that can be set on fire very readily. In fact, it has to be kept under water or some other liquid to keep it from burning. It is used in matches because it burns so easily.

Phosphorus is one of the hundred or so elements that everything else in the world is made of. It is never found pure in nature. It is always joined with other elements in compounds.

Pure phosphorus usually comes in sticks that look as if they were made of yellow wax. But it can be treated so that it is red.

Red phosphorus is not poisonous. Yellow phosphorus is. The workers in match factories used to get a terrible disease called "phossy jaw" from working with yellow phosphorus. Then match companies found that they could use red phosphorus or a compound of phosphorus instead of yellow phosphorus. There is a compound in the heads of strike-anywhere matches. Red phosphorus is used in the striking strip for safety matches.

Scientists have known about phosphorus for about 300 years. An alchemist discovered it while hunting for a substance that could turn metals into gold.

Both plants and animals have to have phosphorus. Plants get it from the soil. Animals get it from their food. We get it from such foods as lean meat, eggs, and cheese. We need phosphorus especially for building good bones and teeth.

To keep their land rich, farmers have to put back into their soil the phosphorus their crops use up. They use fertilizers that have phosphorus in them. Rock phosphate is one of them. Another is bone meal.

In some regions there is a great deal of rock phosphate in the ground. The water in the streams and swamps in parts of southern United States is black because it contains rock phosphate.

The name "phosphorus" means "light-giving." Phosphorus got its name because in damp air it glows with a greenish-white light. (See COMPOUNDS; ELEMENTS; FIRE; MATCHES.)

PHOTOGRAPHY For thousands of years people have made picture records. But up till about 125 years ago all pictures were made by hand with such helps as pens, brushes, paints, and ink. Then the discovery that lenses, chemicals, and light could be used to take pictures was made. Photography began. "Photography" means "writing with light."

Some chemicals change when light strikes them. They are called "light-sensitive" chemicals. These chemicals make photography possible.

The first photographs were taken by a Frenchman named Louis Daguerre. They were called daguerreotypes. Daguerre put a light-sensitive chemical on a plate of copper. The finished picture, too, was on the copper plate. No copies of the picture could be made.

The next advance in photography was coating paper with a light-sensitive chemical. This method is called calotype. Copies could be made, but the method was never popular. Then came the use of glass plates coated with chemicals. Some plates were wet; some of them were dry. Dry plates finally crowded out wet ones. Many copies of the picture could be made when glass plates were used.

Dry plates are still used. But most of today's pictures are taken on film—thin sheets of transparent plastic. George Eastman, an American, got a patent in 1884 on film that could be rolled up. Today's film is, as anyone would expect, much better than that first film.

An ordinary black-and-white photograph is made on a film in this way: The film is put in a camera. In taking the picture, a shutter on the camera lets light shine for a time—perhaps only a hundredth of a second—through the camera lens. The lens makes the light form on the film an image of what is being photographed. The image may be very much smaller than the object being pictured. Otherwise no one could ever take a picture of a house or a big boat or a skyscraper. Before the picture is taken, the photographer focuses the lens of his camera so that the image on the film will be sharp and clear.

POPULAR BOX CAMERAS

Brownie Bull's-eye

Tower "7"

Brownie Hawkeye

Ansco Shur-flash

Brownie Holiday Flash

The chemical on the film is changed where the light strikes it. In the places where the most light strikes it, it is changed most. After the picture is taken, the film must be developed. In the developing, any chemical which has not been changed by light is washed off. The chemical which has been changed is "fixed" so that it will not change any more. In the picture now on the film everything light is dark, and everything dark is light. This kind of picture is called a negative.

From negatives, prints are made. A negative is placed on paper coated with a light-sensitive chemical. It is covered with a plate of glass. Then paper, negative, and glass are held in a strong light. The most light can go through the negative where it is lightest, the least where the negative is darkest. The more light that passes through the negative the more the chemical on the paper is changed. Light and dark are turned around again, and the light and dark are just as they are in whatever is being pictured.

Prints have to be developed and fixed just as negatives do. As many prints as are wanted can be made from one negative.

In the 1930's it became possible to take color photographs. On the film used for them there are layers of different chemicals. Each one of these chemicals is sensitive to a different color.

The film that is used for moving pictures is the same as the film for ordinary pictures. The difference is in the camera. A moving picture camera takes about 24 pictures a second.

Photography is a wonderful hobby. Many exhibits are held, and many prizes are given. But it is much more than fun. Pictures can give us much clearer ideas about many things than words alone can give us. A photograph of a giraffe, for instance, shows us much more clearly what a giraffe looks like than any description can. An encyclopedia with no pictures would need many extra words. Most of the pictures in this encyclopedia were first made by hand. These pictures then had to be photo-

Reproduction of a Color Photograph

graphed in order to reproduce them in all the copies of this book.

Photography plays a very important part in the making of most books. Newspapers and magazines depend greatly on photographs for actual pictures of news events. Film strips are much used in schools. Photographs are a big help in making maps. Banks photograph the checks they cash so that they can keep a record of them. Libraries photograph newspapers on small rolls of film so that they will not have to keep the bulky newspapers on file. The whole great moving picture industry is based on photography. Daguerre probably did not dream how far his invention would go. (See CAMERA; DAGUERREOTYPE; LENSES; LIGHT; MICROFILM; MOTION PICTURES; TELEVISION.)

LENS OPENINGS

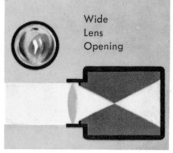

If the opening of the lens is wide, more light shines on the film.

Wide Lens Opening

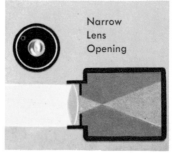

Narrow Lens Opening

If the opening of the lens is narrow, less light is able to reach the film.

LIGHT METERS

Light meters tell how much light is available for taking pictures. Knowing the amount of light, and the type of film in his camera, a photographer can find from a table how wide his camera lens opening should be. The table also tells what shutter speed to use.

NEGATIVE

Developed camera film is called a negative. On a negative, light and dark areas are completely reversed. A print, called a positive, is then made from the negative. On a positive, light and dark are switched around to the way they were in the original scene.

POSITIVE

DARKROOM EQUIPMENT

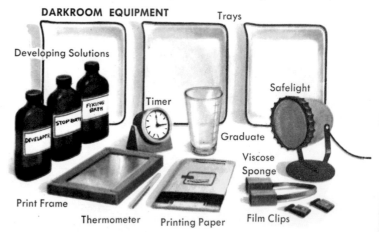

Trays

Developing Solutions

FIXING BATH

STOP BATH

DEVELOPER

Timer

Safelight

Graduate

Viscose Sponge

Print Frame

Thermometer

Printing Paper

Film Clips

PHYSICS Sugar, rubber, glass, yarn, silver, milk, wood, and modeling clay are all common substances. They are easy to tell apart and each one is useful in its own way. No one would think of trying to make an ink bottle out of yarn, or a candle out of sugar. No one would make a bracelet of modeling clay or a dinner plate of silk. No one would try to drink wood or build a fire with milk. No one would make a baseball bat of glass or a baseball of silver. Every substance has what scientists call properties of its own. Yet all substances are alike in some ways. They all weigh something, and they all take up room.

When scientists wish to lump all substances together and talk about them, they use the word "matter." Every substance is a kind of matter. The science of physics is partly a study of matter. It explains why some substances are solids, some liquids, and some gases. It explains how water can evaporate and become a gas as well as how it can freeze and become a solid. It explains why butter melts more easily than iron and where a lump of sugar goes when it is put into hot coffee. It explains why a tire is more likely to blow out on a hot day than on a cold one. It explains many changes that go on around us.

But physics is also a study of energy— of light, heat, sound, electricity, magnetism, of the energy of moving bodies, and of atomic energy. One of the commonest of all questions is "How does it work?" Many, many times we must go to the science of physics to get the answer. And most of the answers have something to do with energy. How does television work? How fast does sound travel? How can a camera take a picture? What are cosmic rays? What are the problems in traveling through outer space? How do waterfalls run power plants? How does an airplane fly? These are a few of the questions that the science of physics answers.

Everyone needs to know something about physics to understand what goes on

around him. It is one of the key sciences. It has taken thousands of scientists to build up the science of physics, just as it has taken thousands of workers to build up every other key science. Some names stand out above the others. The pictures below show a few famous physicists. Among the other great names of all time are Archimedes, Gilbert, Galvani, Henry, and Einstein. (See ATOMS; ELECTRICITY; ENERGY; GRAVITY; HEAT; LIGHT; SOUND; SPACE TRAVEL.)

SOME FAMOUS PHYSICISTS

Galileo

Newton

Faraday

Davy

Roentgen

Fermi

PHYSIOLOGY Why do we need vitamins? How does a potato plant make the starch it stores up in its potatoes? How is our food changed into energy for working and playing? How does a dog keep itself cool? Physiology is the science that answers questions of this kind. It is the study of how the bodies of living things work.

Some physiologists study only how the bodies of human beings work. Some study other animals. Some study plants.

No doctor of either animals or plants can be a good doctor unless he knows a great deal about physiology. Unless, for instance, a doctor knows how our food is digested he will not know what to do for a person with an upset stomach.

There are still many things for physiologists to find out. Many experiments are being carried on. It is not easy for a physiologist to experiment with people. Many physiologists who are trying to find out more about how our bodies work carry on most of their experiments with other animals. Guinea pigs, white rats, rabbits, and dogs are some of the animals they use. The bodies of these animals work enough like ours to give the physiologists some good clues. (See BODY, HUMAN; DIGESTION; ENERGY; VITAMINS.)

PIANO Most of our musical instruments belong in one of these three groups: stringed instruments, wind instruments, and percussion instruments. The piano is not in any one of these groups, for it is partly a stringed instrument and partly a percussion instrument. Inside the large, polished case of the piano are many metal strings stretched over a sounding board. There are also wooden hammers covered with felt which strike the strings when the keys on the keyboard are pushed down.

The keyboard of a standard piano has 88 keys—52 white and 36 black. No two tones from the 88 keys sound exactly alike. A piano has either two or three pedals. By pressing the proper pedal a player can

The clavichord was the forerunner of the piano.

make the tones softer or louder or make them continue longer.

The word "piano" is short for "pianoforte." The instrument was given this name because it could play soft (*piano* in Italian) or loud (*forte* in Italian). One of the oldest pianos in the world is now in the Metropolitan Museum in New York City. It is a grand piano, built in 1720 by an Italian named Bartolomeo Cristofori. Square and upright pianos came later.

The first piano ever built in the United States was made in 1775 in Philadelphia. Soon very good pianos were being made. Two American piano-makers are famous for the fine instruments they built: Jonas Chickering of Boston and Henry Steinway of New York. Today the finest pianos in the world are made in the United States.

The piano is a very good instrument for the home. Music is written for two hands,

Cristofori invented the pianoforte.

four hands, and six hands. A piano player can accompany a singer, a group of singers, or an instrumentalist. He may join with the players of other instruments to make a little orchestra. Or he may play the piano alone for his own and other people's pleasure.

The piano is a good recital instrument, too. More fine music has been written for it than for any other instrument. Some pianists play this music so beautifully that great halls are filled with listeners when they give a recital. (See MUSIC; ORCHESTRA; PERCUSSION INSTRUMENTS; SOUND; STRINGED INSTRUMENTS; WIND INSTRUMENTS.)

The upright piano was popular in the home.

PIGEONS The common pigeon that struts with head a-bobbing in our yards and on our roofs is the pigeon most of us know best. But there are hundreds of other kinds.

As a hobby some people raise pigeons. More than 200 different kinds are raised. Some pigeons are liked for their beautiful feathers. Some do stunts. Some are racers. Pigeon racing is a very old sport.

But not all the pigeons that are raised are raised for fun. Young pigeons, or squabs, are good to eat. They are raised for market just as chickens are. Homing pigeons can be used to carry messages.

Some places are famous for their pigeons. One is the square in front of St. Mark's Cathedral in Venice, Italy. Visitors can buy food to give to the pigeons.

Common Pigeon

Pigeons eat mostly grain and fruit. They need some salt. To drink, pigeons put their beaks deep into the water and draw in all they want. Most birds lift their heads with every swallow.

Pigeons mate for life. Both the father and mother birds sit on the eggs and care for the babies. The parents feed the babies with food they have already digested. This food is called pigeon milk.

The passenger pigeon was once one of our commonest wild birds. Now there are none left. But there are still many wild pigeons. Some of them we call doves. The mourning dove is very much like a small passenger pigeon. Turtledoves are famous for their billing and cooing. They might well be called turtle pigeons instead. (See HOMING PIGEONS; PASSENGER PIGEONS; PETS.)

FANCY SHOW PIGEONS

Fantail

Oriental Frill

Wild Boar

Berkshire

PIGS The dog was the first animal to be tamed. Probably the pig came next. At least pigs were raised before people could write. Pigs are often called hogs. Swine is still another name for them.

The ancestor of the pigs we raise was a wild boar much like the wild boars still found in the forests of Europe. Wild boars are lean and full of fight. They do not look much like any of the pigs in the pictures below. As you can see, young wild boars are striped.

Pigs are raised mostly for their meat and for their fat. The fat is sold as lard. The meat is sold mostly as pork, ham, and bacon. Pigskin is used for such things as gloves and purses.

For various reasons certain religions do not allow their followers to eat pork. The Koran forbids Moslems to eat it because pigs are considered unclean.

Pigs raised chiefly for lard are short and fat. Pigs raised chiefly for meat are longer and leaner. Lard is not as popular for cooking as it used to be. Many kinds of vegetable fats are taking its place. Bacon-type pigs are now more popular than lard-type ones.

The United States leads the world in the raising of pigs. Much corn is raised to be fed to pigs. The two leading corn states —Illinois and Iowa—are also the leaders in hog raising.

Pigs have the reputation of being very dirty animals. But they are not. It is true that they wallow in mud to keep cool and to protect themselves from insects. If they are given clean beds of straw, however, they keep them much cleaner than horses or cattle do.

Pigs have many diseases. Farmers are now crossing pigs of different kinds to try to get hardier ones.

There are some strange pigs. The pygmy pig of India is only a little bigger than a fox terrier. The diving pig of Florida dives under water to get dead fish. The Japanese masked pig has a broad forehead and fleshy ears. (See HYBRIDS.)

Chester White

Hampshire

Poland China

Tamworth

PIKA The pika has several other names. One is "rock rabbit." Another is "little chief hare." The pika does not look much like its relatives, the cottontail and the jackrabbit. With its short ears it looks more like a meadow mouse. But it is larger, and it has no tail that shows.

As one of its names suggests, the pika lives in rocky places. It is found in parts of Asia, Europe, and North America. In the United States it lives above the tree line in the Rocky Mountains. On its feet the pika has little pads which keep it from slipping as it scampers over bare rocks.

The pika's call is a whistle. It is not always easy to tell from what direction the whistle is coming. The pika can "throw" its voice like a ventriloquist.

This little animal hibernates during cold weather. In the fall it gathers a great store of grass and other plant food to last it through the winter. (See RABBITS.)

The pika blends in with his rocky surroundings.

PIKES PEAK In 1803 the United States bought from France nearly a million square miles of land. It reached from the Mississippi River as far west as the Rocky Mountains. This great stretch of land was called the Louisiana Purchase.

Thomas Jefferson was the president of the United States at the time of the purchase. He wanted to know more about the land he had bought. He therefore sent out some men to explore it. One of them was Lieutenant Zebulon Pike.

Autos race to the top of Pikes Peak.

In what is now Colorado, Pike came to the Rocky Mountains. One peak stood out from the others. So far as anyone knows, he was the first white man to see it. It was named Pikes Peak in his honor.

Pikes Peak is the most famous peak in the Rockies. It is not the highest, but it is the easiest of the high peaks to reach. Thousands of people visit it every year. The city of Colorado Springs, with many good hotels, is not far away.

The top of Pikes Peak is 14,110 feet above sea level. Up to about 12,000 feet the sides of the mountain are covered with evergreen forests. Above this point the sides are mostly bare rock. The top of the mountain is flat and broad rather than sharp. The view from the top extends over miles of mountains, plains, lakes, and rivers. It was this view that inspired the author of "America the Beautiful."

Dr. Edwin James was the first person, after the American Indians, to climb to the top of Pikes Peak. He made the climb in 1820. Now every year many people reach the top. But they do not have to climb. They can ride in a car that goes up a cog railway. Or they can ride up in an automobile over a road cut in the mountainside. It was, of course, not easy to build a road and a railroad up a steep mountain nearly three miles high.

At the top of a high mountain the air is much thinner than it is at sea level. The air pressure is not nearly as great either. Visitors to Pikes Peak usually do not wish to stay long at the summit. (See COLORADO; ROCKY MOUNTAINS.)

PILGRIMS The Pilgrims landed in America on a cold day in December, 1620. There were 102 of these English people—men, women, and children. There were no friends to meet them and no houses for shelter. They saw before them the dark forests and the rocky hills of Massachusetts. A foot of snow covered the hard-frozen ground. Behind them stretched the great Atlantic. Their ship, the "Mayflower," had tossed on it for eight weeks. The Pilgrims had suffered crosswinds, fierce storms, and seasickness. But they remembered their purpose in coming—to make a better home for their children and to worship God in their own way.

Without delay the Pilgrims set to work to build a large house from logs cut from the nearby forest. In the house they stored the food and farm tools they had brought with them. They built a few small frame cottages, too. In the cottages and the "common house" they lived and held their church services for the first year. They named their little village Plymouth after the city of Plymouth in England. The village of Plymouth was the first lasting English settlement in New England.

The Pilgrims had suffered much in England because of their religious ideas. They were country people, neighbors in the village and farmlands of Scrooby in northern England. They had separated themselves from the Church of England. The king of England forbade them to hold separate services. He imprisoned some of them. Then the Pilgrims, a few at a time, escaped from England. They crossed the North Sea in Dutch and English ships and settled in Holland. They made their new home in the walled city of Leyden.

They stayed in Holland 12 years, but they were not satisfied. The Dutch had welcomed them and had given them work. The Pilgrims had a church of their own. It still stands in Leyden, and many Americans visit it. But the Pilgrims were English, and longed for a home of their own.

They made plans to leave Holland for faraway America. They borrowed money from some friendly merchants in London. With this sum and their own small savings they rented the "Mayflower." They bought needed supplies for the voyage. The Pilgrims promised to pay back the loan by hard work in the New World.

The first year at Plymouth was filled with hardship and sorrow. Soon after landing many became ill with fever. There were few well persons to care for the sick. About half the company died. The sad little group that lived worked courageously.

They made wise use of land, sea, and forest. In April they planted corn on some old farm lands of Indians who had moved away. Corn was a new grain to the English. They got it from nearby Indians. An Indian named Squanto showed them how to plant it and how to put fish with the seed to enrich the soil. They also planted English wheat and peas. All worked together on one big community farm. They found fishing very good in the rivers and the shallow sea waters. They made excellent boards from the forest trees. They traded English knives and beads with the Indians for beaver skins and corn.

The Pilgrims knew that they must manage to live in this wild new country and also pay their debt to the London merchants. William Bradford, the governor, directed the work. Myles Standish, captain of the little army of fathers and young men, protected the settlement.

The Indians did not hinder the work of the Plymouth people. Some were very helpful. They guided the Pilgrims to fishing spots and to Indians with beaver skins to trade. One day a friendly Indian, Samoset, brought the Indian chief Massasoit and some of his warriors to Plymouth. Massasoit and Governor Bradford made a friendly agreement to live in peace. This peace lasted 50 years. But one day a messenger from a more distant tribe came to Plymouth. He carried a snakeskin filled with arrows. This was a threat of war. Bradford sent it back filled with bullets. He heard no more from these Indians.

After the threat of the snakeskin the settlers built a log fort and a strong log wall around the village of Plymouth. Every night the big gates were locked. Myles Standish and his men stood guard. By day many of the villagers went outside the stockade to work on the farm.

The first autumn harvest was plentiful. Soon wild turkeys and water birds appeared. Deer furnished venison. The Pilgrims in November celebrated the first Thanksgiving. They went to church to thank God. They then had a good dinner. Their guests were Massasoit and his men.

Before the end of November an English ship came with more settlers. It carried away beaver skins, boards, and salted codfish for the merchants of London.

Seven years passed. More English settlers came to Plymouth. They brought cows, hogs, and sheep with them. There was work for all. The Plymouth men and women were repaying the debt well. Then Governor Bradford divided the good farmland beyond the village. He gave to each family a farm suitable to its size. This was a time of great rejoicing. The Pilgrims were well established in the New World. (See COLONIAL LIFE IN AMERICA; MAYFLOWER; THANKSGIVING.)

Feast with Indians

Washing Clothes

Woodcutter

Church Service

Explorers and trappers opened the West.

PIONEER LIFE IN AMERICA For almost 200 years after the founding of Jamestown Americans lived only along the Atlantic coast. The Appalachian Mountains, like a green wall, stood between them and the West. But explorers in time found four natural gateways leading through the mountains. About the time of the Revolutionary War some daring folks began to push through the gateways to the great country beyond. In less than 100 years American pioneers had reached the Pacific Ocean. They had spread their settlements over country many times as large as the original 13 colonies.

The first pioneers were explorers and fur traders. One could tell them by their fringed leather jackets, their bright sashes, and their fur caps. They carried rifles, axes, long knives, and black iron pots. The next

Families in covered wagons followed.

group to go made clearings in the forests. They grew only enough food to feed their families. The third wave of settlers cleared larger spaces for farms. They raised extra crops and livestock to sell.

The first gateway used was Cumberland Gap. It lies where Virginia, Kentucky, and Tennessee meet. Brave leaders like Daniel Boone led farmers and their families along the narrow, steep trail through the gap. They settled in the beautiful meadow and forest land of Kentucky and Tennessee.

Next, pioneers farther north floated down the broad Ohio River to the West. Some went in flatboats that carried family, furniture, and livestock. Some went in the more expensive keelboats, or in canoes. These travelers by water settled here and there on both sides of the river highway.

Flatboats helped in traveling over rivers.

The third gateway was a level trail around the southern end of the Appalachians. Among the Southern pioneers were planters' sons from Virginia and the Carolinas. The planter families moved west in long processions. First went the big carriage swinging on its high springs. It carried the planter with his wife and children. Then there followed wagons of furniture, hunting dogs, and slaves on foot. Planters found land with rich soil and set about growing cotton. They built great houses like their fathers'.

The fourth gateway used was that of the Great Lakes. People found it hard to use

Crude log cabins were built.

dancing and singing. The fiddler played such tunes as "Yankee Doodle," "Pop Goes the Weasel," and "Turkey in the Straw." Men and boys liked shooting matches, foot races, and wrestling.

Settlers near Lake Michigan discovered, beyond the forest in Illinois, a new kind of land. It was covered with tall grass, waist high. There were trees only along the streams. This was prairie land. Pioneers at first avoided the prairies. They said, "Soil that can't grow trees can't grow crops." But late-comers had to take prairie land or none. They found prairie soil very fertile. Prairie

this route until the Erie Canal was built and the steamboat was invented. Then many pioneers followed the lakes westward and settled near their shores.

Most of the land between the Appalachians and the Mississippi River was forest land. Settlers lived a log-cabin life, like their grandfathers in early colonial days. There was hard work for old and young.

But pioneers had many good times. Among their big families there were many weddings. There were quilting bees and spelling matches. The children enjoyed the

Forest land gradually became pasture.

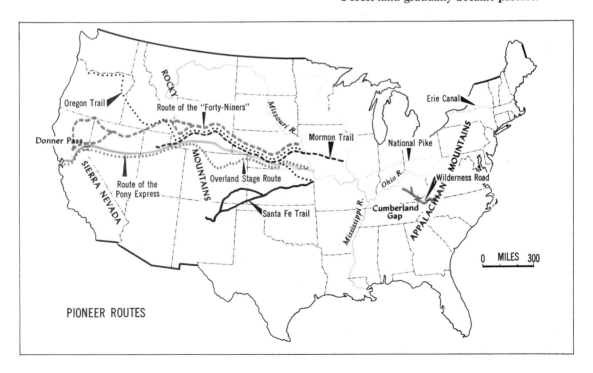

PIONEER ROUTES

Lands were cleared for large farms.

wagons drawn by oxen or mules. They followed the Oregon Trail of the Indians. It led them first over dry, short-grass plains. The sun scorched them. Dust storms bothered them. Sometimes cattle broke away from the drivers. Many people went thirsty. The Indians were hostile. After the Great Plains the trail led over rainy and snowy passes in the mountains. But the Oregon Country, when they arrived, was green with tall forest and meadow. The weather was mild. These pioneers became farmers, lumbermen, and salmon fishermen.

Farther south along the coast in southern California American sailors on voyages found a dry and sunny country. They discovered, too, many little green valleys facing the sea. Each valley held a small Spanish settlement called a mission. In each mission Spanish priests and hundreds of Indians lived. They had built a mission church and a village and had laid out great ranches. The church and the houses had walls of adobe and roofs of red tile. Away from the village stretched orchards of olive and orange trees and great fields of wheat. Cattle grazed on grassy slopes. Rains were light and came only in winter. The Indians irrigated orchards and gardens with water from mountain streams. American pio-

farms gave big crops of corn and wheat. Prairie grass was good for cattle. But the prairie farmers had troubles, too. The great grass roots made the ground hard to plow. And there were often prairie fires. Men, women, and children had to work together to beat out the flames and to plow strips of bare ground to stop the fires. In winter, blizzards blew snow into the cabins.

Settlements in the forest land were still young when some pioneers reached the Oregon Country in the Pacific Northwest. At the big bend of the Missouri River, before it joins the Mississippi, pioneers gathered to make ready for the 2,000-mile journey. They set out in groups in canvas-covered

Often Indian tribes swooped down on covered wagon camps.

neers liked the mild, sunny climate. They built adobe houses, too, and irrigated their farmlands just as the Indians did.

One of these American settlers discovered gold in northern California. Soon thousands of Americans, the "forty-niners," rushed to California. They came by covered wagon and by ship. Only a few grew rich in the gold fields. The gold gave out. Miners then started growing wheat.

The last part of the country to be settled was the Great Plains. Pioneers had hurried over the plains on their way westward. The plains were very dry. Early, however, some pioneers from the Ohio River settlements had moved to the plains of Texas. There they found Spanish cattlemen with great ranches. The Americans learned the cattle business from them. The pioneers dressed like Spanish cowboys and learned to ride tough little Spanish horses that could live on dry bunchgrass. They learned to use the lariat, to round up the cattle, and then to brand them. Later, railroads thrust their way westward into the plains. Then the cowmen drove herds of cattle from Texas northward to the railroad "cow towns" for shipment to the East.

Farmer pioneers came to the plains on the railroads. There was little timber on the plains. The farmers cut sod into three-foot bricks. With them, they built little cabins with dirt floors. Often children could pick sunflowers from the grassy roofs of their homes. A sod house was cool in summer and warm in winter. The sod-house farmers grew much wheat on the dry plains. They became prosperous. Then they could afford frame houses.

The movement of pioneers to the west is often called the Westward Movement. The pioneers learned to suit their ways of living to many kinds of country. They learned to respect everyone who was brave and willing to work. They believed that everyone should have an equal chance in the New World. (See BOONE, DANIEL; COVERED WAGON; PLAINS; PRAIRIE.)

The Barbary pirates sailed the Mediterranean Sea.

PIRATES Captain Kidd, Henry Morgan, Blackbeard: These names are enough to send shivers up and down one's spine. For they are the names of famous pirates.

Pirates are sea robbers. There were pirates almost as early as there were ships.

Four hundred years ago there were many pirates in the Mediterranean Sea. They were sometimes called the "sea wolves of the Mediterranean." Another name for them was corsairs. The most famous of the corsairs was Khair-ed-Din. His nickname was Barbarossa, which means "red beard." In his raids he took many captives and treated them very cruelly. After his death, legends said, he could not lie quiet in his grave. He had to be buried several times.

In the first half of the 17th century a Chinese pirate named Cheng sailed up and down the coast of China, robbing merchant ships on their way from the Far East to

Cheng's pirate fleet robbed European merchants.

Buccaneer ships roamed the shipping lanes.

Europe. He was very vain, and his vanity brought about his undoing. The emperor of China invited him to the royal court. Cheng, very much pleased, accepted the invitation. But when he arrived he was seized and beheaded.

After the Spaniards conquered a large part of the New World, pirates swarmed the waters around the West Indies. They lay in wait for Spanish ships carrying home gold and silver. These pirates were called buccaneers. Their flag was the Jolly Roger. It was black, with a white skull and crossbones on it. The flag, they said, was to "strike terror on" everyone who saw it.

The boldest of the buccaneers was Henry Morgan. His band of pirates robbed ships and cities along the coast of huge amounts of treasure. In one of his daring raids he had 37 ships and 2,000 men under him. But at last his men accused him of not dividing the booty fairly. He then gave up the life of a pirate. He died in his bed—something very few pirates did.

Captain Kidd is the most famous of all pirates. Strange as it seems, he may not have wanted to be a pirate at all. For years he was an honest seaman. Then in 1695 the king of England chose him to try to capture some of the pirates who were then the terror of the New England coast. Kidd set sail from New York. For months nothing was heard from him. Then ugly stories about him began coming back. Instead of

capturing pirate ships, the stories said, Captain Kidd had turned pirate himself. When at last he came back to New York he was arrested and sent to England. There he was tried and hanged. He claimed that his crew had forced him to turn pirate. No one will ever know the truth.

Blackbeard's real name was Edward Teach. He was cruel even for a buccaneer. When he was finally killed in a battle at sea, his head was brought to Virginia and put up on a pole for everyone to see.

Of all pirates, Bartholomew Roberts probably came closest to being like the pirates in storybooks. He wore a cocked hat covered with plumes. His breeches and waistcoat were made of heavy silk. Around his neck there hung a heavy gold chain with a diamond cross. For fighting he always had with him a sword and two pairs of pistols. He was one of the last of the famous pirates along the American shores.

Visitors to New Orleans are almost sure to hear of Jean Laffite, the "pirate of the Gulf." Laffite was really a smuggler rather than a pirate. He won the good will of Americans by helping defend New Orleans from the British in the War of 1812.

Pirates did not obey the laws of any country. But every pirate band had its rules, and woe to the pirate who broke them! Marooning was one punishment. Marooning meant leaving a person on a desolate island with only a gun, a pinch of powder,

Pirates often taught parrots to talk and sing.

a few bullets, and a jug of water. Cutting off an ear was another common punishment. Making a person "walk the plank" was still another. To walk the plank a person was blindfolded and made to walk over the side of the ship on a board. When he reached the end of the plank he fell in the sea and drowned. Pirates were cruel to one another as well as to their captives.

There are many legends of buried pirate treasure. Certainly some pirates did bury chests of treasure that they were never able to come back to get. Some chests have been found. But not nearly enough buried treasure has been dug up to pay for all the time people have spent hunting for it.

Pirates are almost a thing of the past. For many years there have been none except near the east coast of Asia. Perhaps there are none there now. (See CARIBBEAN SEA; CRETE; VIKINGS.)

Cattle were herded over the plains to market.

PLAIN Stretches of almost level lowland are called plains. Along many rivers there are narrow flood plains. There are other plains that cover thousands of square miles. Every continent has its plains.

In the United States, the Great Plains reach from western Minnesota, Iowa, Missouri, and Arkansas westward to the Rockies. In places the plains are so nearly flat that in the days of steam locomotives smoke from a train could be seen for 25 miles. The Great Plains slope up gently toward the

west. Near the Rockies they are far higher than most plains. But they are low compared with the Rocky Mountains. White men found there great herds of pronghorn and bison. The plains became the land of ranches and cowboys. (See BISON; PIONEER LIFE IN AMERICA; RANCHES; ROCKY MOUNTAINS.)

The Morrison Planetarium is in San Francisco.

PLANETARIUM The machine in the picture throws a picture of the night sky on the ceiling of a great dome-shaped building where hundreds of people can sit and watch. It is called a planetarium. This wonderful machine shows how the stars seem to move across the sky and how the planets wander among the stars. It is so remarkable that it can show how the sky looked at any time during the past 10,000 years. It can show, too, how the sky will look on any night for 10,000 years to come.

The first planetarium was built in Munich, Germany. Now there are planetariums in many cities. The one in the picture is in the Morrison Planetarium in San Francisco. There are several other famous planetariums in the United States.

There are also smaller, less complicated planetariums that show the motions of the stars. These planetariums do not need a special building. They come equipped with dome-shaped enclosures big enough to hold small groups of people. There are even smaller "toy" planetariums that people can use at home to study the stars on their own ceilings. (See ASTRONOMY; PLANETS; SOLAR SYSTEM; STARS; UNIVERSE.)

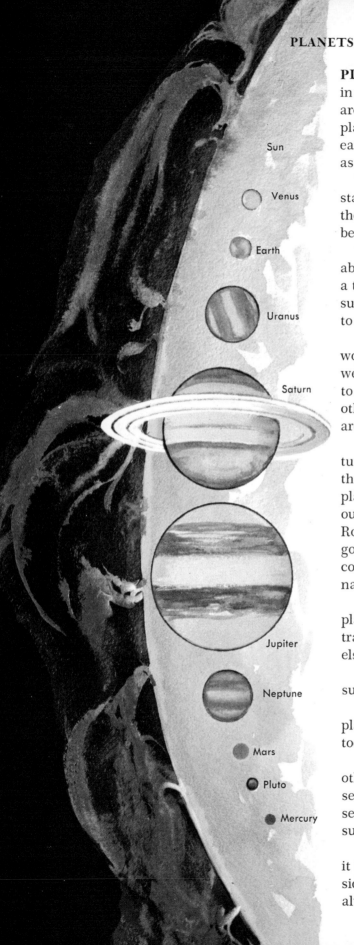

Sun

Venus

Earth

Uranus

Saturn

Jupiter

Neptune

Mars

Pluto

Mercury

PLANETS Some of the brightest "stars" in the sky at night are not really stars. They are planets. The earth is a planet. The other planets are big balls somewhat like the earth. They all travel around the sun just as the earth does.

The planets we see in the sky look like stars. But they do not give off any light of their own as stars do. They are bright only because the sun is shining on them.

There are nine planets that we know about. We cannot see all of them without a telescope. Some are so far away from the sun that they are not bright enough for us to see with our eyes alone.

The word "planet" comes from a Greek word which means "wanderer." The planets were given this name because they seem to wander from one group of stars to another. They seem to wander because they are traveling around the sun.

Mercury, Venus, Mars, Jupiter, and Saturn were known long before anyone knew that the earth is a wanderer, too. These five planets are the ones that can be seen without a telescope. The ancient Greeks and Romans named them for their gods and goddesses. The planets that have been discovered since Roman times have been named for other Greek and Roman gods.

Some of the planets have moons. As the planets travel around the sun their moons travel around them just as our moon travels around the earth.

Each planet has its own path around the sun. This path is called the planet's orbit.

The chart on the next page names the planets in their order from the sun. It gives, too, some important facts about them.

Mercury travels faster than any of the other planets. It was named for the messenger of the gods. This planet is hard to see. It is so much closer than we are to the sun that it is usually lost in the sun's glare.

No one like us could live on Mercury. As it travels around the sun, it keeps the same side always toward the sun. One side is always light. It is far too hot for living things of the kinds we know. The other side is always dark, and very, very cold.

Venus was named for the goddess of beauty. In the night sky it shines more brightly than any true star. Of all the heavenly bodies only the sun and the moon are brighter. Venus can never be seen in the middle of the night. Sometimes it shines in the evening in the western sky. Then it is called the evening star. Sometimes it shines before sunrise in the eastern sky. Then it is called the morning star.

Venus is always covered with clouds. No one has ever been able to look through the clouds and see the surface. No one is sure whether Venus keeps the same side always toward the sun. Scientists do not believe that people like us could live there.

Mars looks like a red star as we see it in the sky. It was named for the god of war. If we look through a telescope we see dark patches on this planet. Perhaps the patches are swamps in which plants are growing. At the poles of Mars there are white caps. They may be fog-covered fields of snow.

Through a telescope some people have seen straight lines on Mars. One idea about these lines is that they are wide bands of plants growing along water channels. But not all scientists see the lines.

No people like us could live on Mars. There is not enough oxygen. Neither is there enough water.

Jupiter was named for the king of the gods. It is by far the largest planet. It is so big that, if it were hollow, there would be room for 1,000 earths inside it. It looks like a very bright star as we see it in the sky. Through a telescope one can see bands of cloud around Jupiter.

No earth people could possibly live on this giant planet. Its atmosphere would suffocate humans. Besides, Jupiter and all the planets beyond it are far too cold.

A picture of Saturn taken through a telescope does not look at all like pictures of the other planets. Saturn has rings of tiny particles around it. Perhaps one of Saturn's moons once came too near the big planet and was pulled to pieces. Or the particles may be mostly crystals of ice. Saturn was named for the god of harvests.

Uranus was not discovered until 1781. It was named for the god of the heavens. People with very good eyesight can sometimes see Uranus without a telescope.

Neptune was discovered in 1846. It was named for the god of the sea. No one can see Neptune without a telescope.

Pluto was the last planet to be discovered. Its discovery was announced in 1930. It was named for the god of the underworld. Even through a powerful telescope Pluto is very dim. It is so cold that, if it had any air, the air would be frozen.

If a person could visit all the planets he would find that he would weigh much more on some of them than on others. His weight would not be the same because the gravity on all the planets is not the same. Imagine cutting your weight in two by going to Mars and making it 2½ times as much by going to Jupiter! (See EARTH; GRAVITY; MOON; SOLAR SYSTEM.)

NAME	DIAMETER (in miles)	DISTANCE FROM SUN (in millions of miles)	YEAR (time needed for journey around sun)	DAY (time needed in turning on axis)	MOONS
Mercury	3,000	36	88 days	88 days	0
Venus	7,600	67	225 days	30 days (?)	0
Earth	7,900	93	365¼ days	23hr. 56m.	1
Mars	4,200	142	687 days	24hr. 37m.	2
Jupiter	87,000	483	12 yrs.	9hr. 50m.	12
Saturn	71,500	886	29½ yrs.	10hr. 14m.	9
Uranus	29,500	1,783	84 yrs.	10hr. 48m.	5
Neptune	26,800	2,791	165 yrs.	15hr. 48m.	2
Pluto	3,600	3,671	248 yrs.	6½ days (?)	0

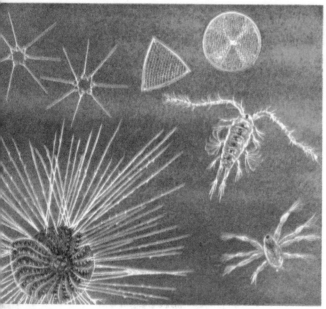

Plankton is made up of countless billions of plants and animals.

Diatoms   Copepod   Smelt   Mackerel   Tuna

The food of many animals of the sea can be traced back to the diatoms.

PLANKTON The word "plankton" comes from a Greek word meaning "drifting" or "free-floating." Plankton is made up of tiny floating plants and animals. It is found in lakes, streams, and oceans from the arctic to the equator. Some of the tiny plants and animals in it are too small to be seen without a microscope. Plankton in the ocean is sometimes called "sea soup."

Plankton is the basic diet of young fishes. It is in fact the only food of many fishes and even of some whales. The menhaden, or "fatback," a salt-water fish, is of great value as a source of oil, which it gets from plankton. Plankton is able to float partly because of the tiny oil drops in the bodies of the little plants and animals. Most of the plants in plankton are algae.

By far the most numerous and interesting of the algae are the diatoms. They have shells that fit together like a pillbox and have beautiful designs.

The most numerous plankton animals are one-celled protozoa and rotifers, or wheel animals. The largest are tiny shrimplike crustaceans. One kind, called krill, forms the chief food of the huge blue whale. (See ALGAE; CRUSTACEANS; DIATOMS; GAME FISHES; FISHES; PROTOZOA; WHALES.)

PLANT BREEDING Tangelos, cauliflower, and some of the other kinds of plants we raise never grew wild. There were none until long after people first planted gardens and orchards. Wheat did once grow wild, as did apples, carrots, cotton, and many of the other plants we raise. But these plants are now much better for our purposes than their wild ancestors. The work of getting new and better kinds of plants is called plant breeding.

When a plant breeder starts work, he has in mind the kind of plant he would like to get. He may want a new fruit that looks like an apple and tastes like a pear. He may want an orange tree that can stand cold weather. He may want a flower of a new

Cultivated Plum

Wild Plum

color or a grain that is not likely to get a disease. He may want a seedless cucumber or a berry that will bear all summer.

To get the kind of plant he wants, a plant breeder may cross two plants. The tangelo is a cross between the tangerine and the grapefruit. But a plant breeder could not hope to get a peach as large as a watermelon by crossing those two fruits. Only plants that are closely related can be crossed. And not all of them can be. The breeder also watches closely for sports among his plants. A plant sport is a plant that by chance is quite different from the plant it came from. Most sports are not worth saving. But some are.

Careful selection is another way of improving plants. A plant breeder chooses his seed for the next year's planting from the best plants in this year's crop.

Plant breeders may have many disappointments. But the seed catalogues each year show us that they accomplish a great deal. (See BURBANK, LUTHER; FLOWER; FRUITS; GRAFTING; HEREDITY; HYBRIDS; VEGETABLES.)

To get the best corn, growers combine the best features of four different kinds. But the hybrid corn will not yield as good a second crop. The grower has to repeat the crossing process yearly.

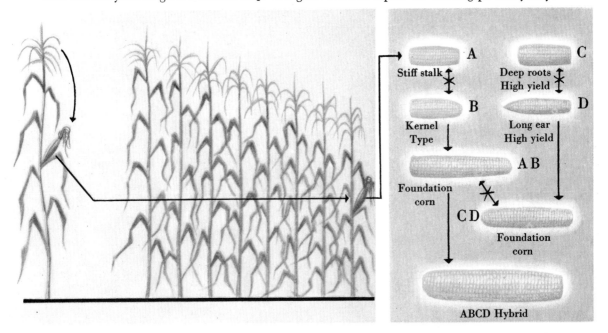

Maple Tree

This year's sap was made by last year's leaves.

PLANT FACTORIES In our big cities there are thousands of factories. But these factories are not the most important in the world. The most important factories are in our fields and gardens and orchards. They are the green plants we raise there.

Green plants are the most important factories because we could not live without them. They make food.

Of course, meat does not grow on plants. But it comes from plant-eating animals. Bread and butter do not grow on plants. But bread is made from flour, which comes from the seeds of plants. And butter is made from milk, which comes from animals that eat plants. Some of the fish we eat, eat little fish. The little fish in turn eat smaller animals that eat plants. All our

food except water and salt can be traced back to green plants.

We are not the only ones that depend on plants for food. All animals do. A world without plants would be a world without animals. Green plants make food out of water and soil and air. They can make food because of a wonderful green dye in them. Scientists call this green dye "chlorophyll." This name means "leaf green." One of the kinds of food green plants make is sugar. They make it out of nothing but water and carbon dioxide. Carbon dioxide is one of the gases in the air.

Water is part oxygen. Carbon dioxide is part oxygen, too. When plants are making sugar, they get more oxygen than they need. They throw some of it away. It is lucky for us that they do. For oxygen is the part of the air we have to have. All the oxygen in the air might have been used up long ago if green plants did not keep on throwing it away.

A plant's wonderful green dye is not scattered evenly all through the plant. It is found, as a rule, in tiny green bodies. Scientists call them "chloroplasts." In plants that have leaves most of the tiny green bodies are in the leaves. They are the "machines" of the plant factories.

No machine will do any work unless there is some kind of energy to make it do so. The machines in green plants get their energy from sunlight. At night, unless strong artificial light is used, green plants do not make sugar.

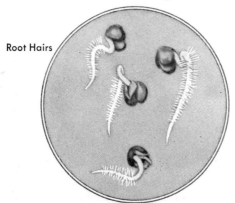

Root Hairs

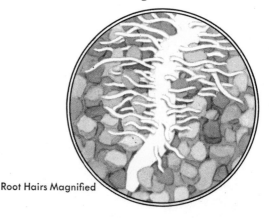

Root Hairs Magnified

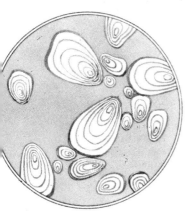

Grains of Starch

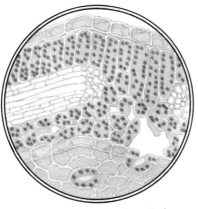

Bit of Leaf at Right Magnified

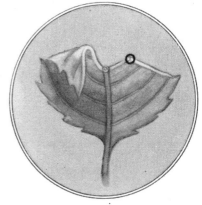

Leaf Cut Across

There is always carbon dioxide in the air, but it has to get inside the plant before it can be used. It has to reach the tiny green bodies. Leaves have skin on the outside. In it are tiny openings, or pores. Carbon dioxide comes in through these pores.

The water usually has a much longer trip to take to reach the green bodies. In an apple tree, for instance, it soaks into hairs on the roots of the tree. Then it travels up through the roots in tiny tubes. It goes from them to water tubes in the trunk of the tree. These carry it to the branches. Tubes in the branches carry it to the veins of the leaves. The veins carry it to the little green bodies.

Of course, green plants are making sugar for themselves, not for us. After they have made the sugar, it travels to all the parts of the plant that need it.

Once sugar is made, a plant can make the other foods it needs. It can make starch very easily out of sugar. It can make fats and other foods, too. To make some foods it needs minerals from the soil. Water brings the minerals into the plant.

Most green plants make food faster than they use it up. They have some to store away. They may store it in their roots or stems or seeds. They may store it in their leaves or fruits. Whenever we eat a carrot or an apple or an ear of corn we are really robbing a plant storehouse.

There is never a strike in a plant food factory. A green plant factory runs day in and day out if it can get the materials it has to have and the energy it needs—if, that is, there is plenty of water and carbon dioxide and sunshine.

We depend on green plants for food. They manufacture many other things, too, some of them very useful. We have plants to thank for rubber, turpentine, linseed oil, resin, and chicle for chewing gum. We have them to thank for vegetable dyes and for spices. And we have them to thank for quinine, camphor, and many other drugs. Even if we did not depend on plants for so much of our food, they would still be very important factories. (See AIR; CARBON DIOXIDE; ENERGY; FOOD; FRUITS; LEAVES; MAPLE SUGAR; MINERALS; OXYGEN; VEGETABLES.)

Oxygen Rising from Green Plant

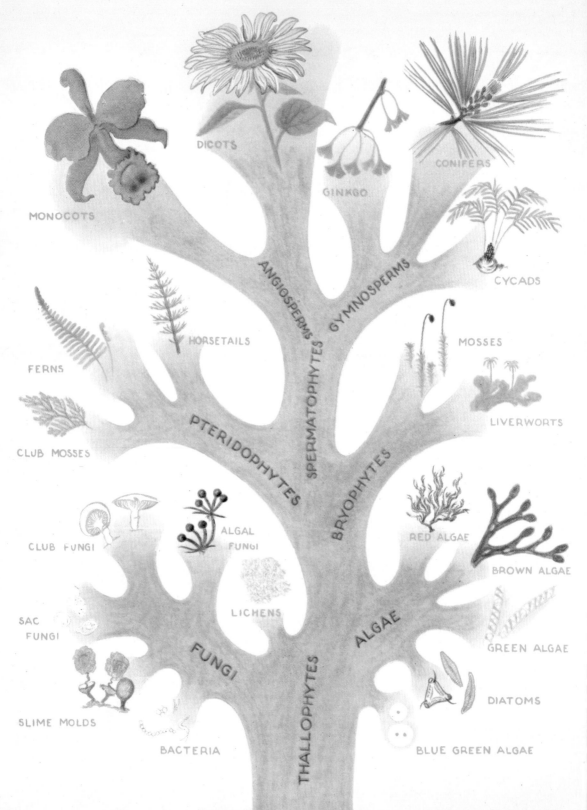

MONOCOTS

DICOTS

GINKGO

CONIFERS

CYCADS

ANGIOSPERMS

GYMNOSPERMS

HORSETAILS

FERNS

MOSSES

LIVERWORTS

CLUB MOSSES

PTERIDOPHYTES

SPERMATOPHYTES

BRYOPHYTES

CLUB FUNGI

ALGAL FUNGI

LICHENS

RED ALGAE

BROWN ALGAE

SAC FUNGI

GREEN ALGAE

ALGAE

FUNGI

THALLOPHYTES

DIATOMS

SLIME MOLDS

BACTERIA

BLUE GREEN ALGAE

ANCESTRAL PROTOPHYTA

PLANT KINGDOM In the whole world there are more than 300,000 different kinds of plants. Some plants are so tiny that they cannot be seen without a powerful microscope. Other plants grow to be huge. A tree, which of course is a plant, may be so big that it has enough wood to build a whole village. The tiniest plants are smaller than the tiniest animals. The biggest plants are bigger than the biggest animals.

Many plants are green, but not all are. Thousands of kinds do not have any green coloring. Green plants can make food for themselves with the help of sunshine. Almost all plants that are not green have to live on food green plants have made.

Some plants, even though they can make food for themselves, catch insects for "dessert." But eating meat is certainly not the rule among plants.

Some plants have beautiful flowers. Others have flowers that are not at all showy. Still others have no flowers.

Almost every part of the world has its green plants. There are none in the saltiest and the coldest and the driest regions. There are none in the deepest parts of the sea, where it is always dark. But at least a few kinds of plants are fitted for living everywhere else.

Many plants live for only one season. Some live for an even shorter time. But some kinds live for hundreds or even thousands of years. The oldest plants are far older than the oldest animals.

There are many ways of dividing plants into different groups. They can all be divided into groups according to the amount of water they need. They can be divided into groups according to their size, how long they live, or how they get their food. They can also be divided into groups according to the way they are built and how they produce new plants.

If this last way of dividing plants is used, there are four big groups. The chart shows the four groups. It shows, too, some of the divisions of these groups. The four groups are the thallus plants (thallophytes), the mosslike plants (bryophytes), the fernlike plants (pteridophytes), and the seed plants (spermatophytes).

"Thallus" means a plant body without true roots, stems, or leaves. The group of thallus plants is made up of the algae, the fungi, and the lichens. The thallus plants are simpler than those in the other groups. They are more like the plants that first lived on the earth. Some of them are made up of only a single cell. Most algae live in the water. All the seaweeds and pond scums are algae. Yeasts, molds, mushrooms, and bacteria are fungi. None of the fungi are green. Lichens are part algae and part fungi. The thallus plants have no flowers. They do not have seeds. They produce new plants in several different ways. In some cases a one-celled plant merely divides into two plants.

The group of mosslike plants is made up of the true mosses and the liverworts. They are all small plants. So far as we know, they always have been small. Almost everybody has seen moss growing. Liverworts are not nearly so common. They grow in damp places such as the walls of ravines. The mosslike plants do not have flowers or seeds. They have spores instead of seeds.

The group of fernlike plants includes the ferns, the club mosses, and the horsetails. Millions of years ago, in the Coal Age, there were many tree ferns, tree horsetails, and tree club mosses. Now most of the plants in the group are rather small. There are still some tree ferns in warm regions. The plants in this group have no flowers or seeds. They, too, have spores.

As their name tells, the seed plants produce seeds. In this group there are some plants that bear their seeds in cones. Among them are the pines and firs and spruces. But most of the seed plants produce their seeds by means of flowers. For millions of years there were no flowering plants at all. After they finally appeared they almost took over the earth. More than half of all the kinds of plants on earth are flowering plants.

People did not appear on the earth until after the flowering plants. This is good, for people would have had a very hard time getting enough to eat without flowering plants. Almost all the food we get from plants come from plants with flowers.

In the chart of the plant kingdom, the simplest plants are at the bottom. The seed plants are on the top branches. The plant kingdom is drawn as a tree to bring out the idea that all the plants of today have come from the very simple plants that first lived on the earth. (See ALGAE; BOTANY; CLUB MOSSES; CONIFERS; FERNS; FLOWER; FLOWER FAMILIES; FUNGI; HORSETAILS; LICHENS; LIVERWORTS; MOSSES; SEEDS; TREES.)

PLANT LICE Many plant stems are crowded with tiny insects called aphids. Another name for these tiny insect pests is "plant lice."

Aphids do not move about much. Most of them have no wings. They get their food by sucking the juice from plants.

These small insects multiply fast. It takes about ten days for an aphid to grow up. In one summer there may be a dozen generations. The oldest aphid on a plant may have great-great-great-great-great-great-great-great-great-great-great-grandchildren around her. Aphids multiply so fast that they would kill all the green plants on earth if they did not have enemies. Aphis-lions and ladybird beetles are among their enemies. These insects eat aphids. Some birds eat them, too. Farmers and gardeners kill many aphids with poison.

Some aphids are called "ant cows." They furnish a sweet juice called honeydew, which ants eat. Ants "milk" their "cows" by stroking them with their feelers. Ants keep the aphids in the ant nests during the winter and carry them out to "pasture" in the spring when the weather is warm. The pasture is some part of a green plant.

PLASTICS Many, many of the things we have are made of plastics. Dishes, knives and forks, shower curtains, seat covers, raincoats, squeeze bottles, toys, brushes, beads, buttons, table tops, dress bags, food covers, music records—these are some of the many ways in which plastics are used. Even the bodies of some cars are made of plastic. Plastics are fast taking the place of wood, leather, glass, cloth, and metal. Besides, they are being used to glue other materials together. The thin sheets of wood in plywood are held together by a plastic glue. Plastics are also used as a coating on other materials. Paper book covers may be given a coating of plastic. Copper wire may have a plastic jacket.

Plastics get their name because they can be pressed or molded into shape. "Plastic" means "moldable." Plastics are made out of such things as air, cotton, water, waste wood, limestone, and coal tar.

The first plastic was celluloid. It was invented in 1869. At that time all billiard balls were made of ivory. Ivory was hard to get, and it was expensive. A maker of billiard balls offered a prize to anyone who could find something else that could be

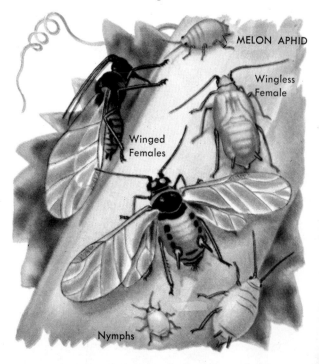

MELON APHID

Wingless Female

Winged Females

Nymphs

USES OF PLASTICS

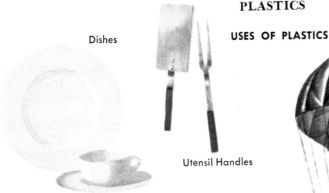

Dishes

Utensil Handles

Nylon Parachute

Nylon Stockings

Billiard Ball

Cup

Comb

Eyeglass Frames

Book Protector

used to make billiard balls. A printer of Albany, N. Y., decided that he would try for the prize. He succeeded in making celluloid. He made it from short fibers of cotton, camphor, and nitric acid. Celluloid was not good for billiard balls. But many uses were found for this new material. For many things it was a good substitute for ivory, bone, hard rubber, and glass.

There was not much interest in making other plastics for about 50 years. Then Bakelite was invented. Since that time plastics have come thick and fast.

Plastics have long names that tell what chemicals are in them. Besides, the companies that make them often give them brand names. Bakelite, Vinylite, Pyralin, and Lustron are some of the brand names.

All plastics can be divided into two groups. Some of them have to be heated to harden them. These are called "thermosetting" plastics. They cannot be remolded. The others are heated to make them soft enough to mold. They must then be cooled to make them hard. These are called "thermoplastic." They can be remolded.

Every boy and girl reading this book probably has plastic on in some form or another —buttons, pens, eyeglass frames, belts, or jewelry. Even the tips on shoelaces are made of plastic.

Plastic products are popular partly because they are inexpensive and clean. As the picture shows, moreover, they can be made in very gay colors. (See AIR; CHEMISTRY; COAL; COAL TAR; COTTON; NYLON; WATER; WOOD.)

Plateaus are high, flat stretches of land.

PLATEAU A plateau is a stretch of rather level land that is high above the sea. It is somewhat like the top of a great table. For this reason plateaus are sometimes called tablelands.

Most plateaus are near mountains. Some of them have mountains crossing them.

One of the plateaus in the United States is called the Columbia Plateau. It is in the Northwest. This plateau was built up by great floods of lava. Some 15 million years ago lava poured out from huge cracks there. It spread over thousands and thousands of square miles. The lava covered the hills, and then it covered most of the mountains. In places it was a mile deep. The tops of the highest mountains rose above it like islands in a sea. Later the lava hardened into solid rock.

Not all plateaus were formed in this way. Some were simply pushed up when the mountains near them were made.

One of the very high plateaus is the plateau of Tibet. There are other very high ones along the Andes Mountains. Much of Mexico is plateau. So is most of Iceland. The great Colorado Plateau is in southwestern United States. It is in this plateau that the Colorado River has carved the Grand Canyon.

Deep valleys are found in many plateaus. In fact, as thousands of years go by, streams may cut up a plateau into hills high enough to be called mountains. (See GRAND CANYON; TIBET.)

PLATINUM In the first 100 years after Columbus discovered America, the Spaniards conquered Mexico and a large part of South America. They were most interested in the gold they found. They took the great stores of gold of the Indian rulers. But they wanted more. They discovered that they could wash gold from the sand in some South American rivers. In with the gold they found little lumps of a gray metal. They did not bother to save them. They did not guess that the metal in the little lumps was much scarcer than gold and would someday be worth much more.

This gray metal was not given its name for nearly 200 years. Then it was brought to Europe and named platinum. "Platinum" comes from the Spanish word *platina,* which means "little silver."

Today platinum is sometimes called the king of metals. It is easy to work. It does not rust. It can stand terrific heat. No single acid will eat it. And it is very tough. It is so tough that it can be made into wire almost too fine to imagine. Some platinum wire is so amazingly fine that it would take 25,000 strands of it to make a strand as big around as a hair.

A great deal of jewelry is made of platinum. But by no means all the platinum that is mined goes into jewelry. A large part of it goes into such things as these: radio and television sets, X-ray machines, spark plugs for airplanes, sun lamps, crucibles for melting glass and rock, and machines for spinning nylon and rayon and glass yarn. Dentists use platinum to fasten in false teeth. Doctors use platinum to help hold broken bones together.

The United States uses more platinum than any other country in the world. But almost all of it must be imported from other lands. South Africa has some platinum. So do some of the countries of South America. But the countries with the greatest amounts are Canada and the Soviet Union. (See ELEMENTS; JEWELRY; LAMPS AND LIGHTING; METALS.)

POISONOUS PLANTS The number three and the color white are danger signals in the woods. For poison ivy has three leaflets on each leaf and white berries. Poison ivy is one of the most common and most feared of the many poisonous plants. Virginia creeper is often confused with it. But Virginia creeper has five leaflets on each leaf and blue berries. It is not poisonous.

Poison ivy may grow either as a bush or as a vine that climbs over fences and up trunks of trees. In the summer its leaves are a shiny green. They turn a beautiful red in the fall.

People get poisoned by just touching poison ivy. The poisoning is caused by oil which is in all parts of the plant—even in the pollen of its flowers. Some people are poisoned by poison ivy much more easily than others. Some have only a slight itching while others have severe swelling and soreness from it.

Poison sumac is another plant that is poisonous to the touch. It grows on lowlands and in swamps. When full grown it is a bush about 25 feet high. Its berries, like poison ivy berries, are white. In the fall the leaves of poison sumac are of such a brilliant red color that they tempt people to pick them.

Some poisonous plants are poisonous to eat, not to touch. Among them are pokeberry, bittersweet, nightshade, and Jimson weed. Their fruits, roots, or berries are sometimes eaten by mistake.

Certain kinds of mushrooms are also very poisonous to eat. Not many people are able to tell which mushrooms are poisonous and which are not. It is easy to make a mistake and eat poisonous ones. The death angel and the fly mushroom are among the most dangerous.

Cattle and horses sometimes eat poisonous plants which grow in their pastures. Water hemlock is one of the most poisonous of these pasture plants.

Some poisonous plants are helpful. Valuable drugs of many kinds are made from plant poisons. (See DRUGS.)

Death Angel

Pokeberries

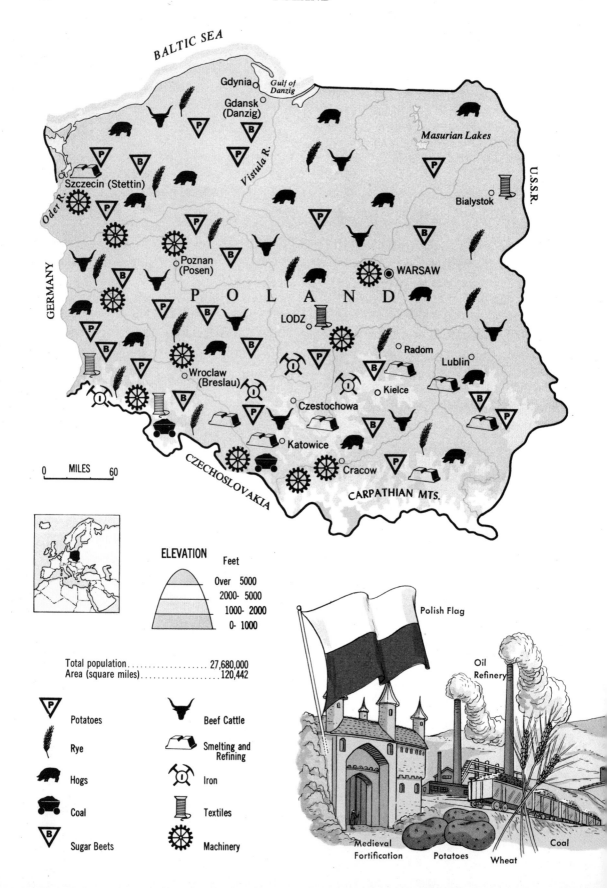

BALTIC SEA

Gdynia

Gulf of Danzig

Gdansk (Danzig)

Masurian Lakes

Vistula R.

U.S.S.R.

Bialystok

Szczecin (Stettin)

Oder R.

GERMANY

Poznan (Posen)

P O L A N D

WARSAW

LODZ

Radom

Lublin

Wroclaw (Breslau)

Kielce

Czestochowa

Katowice

Cracow

CZECHOSLOVAKIA

CARPATHIAN MTS.

0   MILES   60

ELEVATION   Feet

Over 5000
2000- 5000
1000- 2000
0- 1000

Total population 27,680,000
Area (square miles) 120,442

Potatoes   Beef Cattle

Rye   Smelting and Refining

Hogs   Iron

Coal   Textiles

Sugar Beets   Machinery

Polish Flag

Oil Refinery

Medieval Fortification   Potatoes   Wheat   Coal

POLAND Today, Poland is one of the larger countries of Europe. As the map shows, this country now has much coast along the Baltic Sea to its north. One of Europe's great rivers, the Oder, forms much of Poland's western boundary. The country's southern border is mountainous. And to the east, Poland's neighbor is the Soviet Union. Since World War II, Poland has had a communist government.

As signs on the map for rye, potatoes, sugar beets, cattle, and hogs show, Poland has many farms and farmers. It has forests, too. Most farm homes are built of whitewashed logs or boards and are thatched with straw. Most farms are small, and most farmers make only a poor living. But better ways of farming with better tools now seem to be spreading.

On the map there are many signs for cities, coal, iron, smelting and refining, and factories in south and west Poland. Many people there live in cities. In and near the cities are mines and many factories.

The Poland of today is a new Poland. For about 125 years before 1919 there was no Poland on maps of Europe. But Warsaw, Poland's capital today, had been the capital, too, of a Poland that was a kingdom of long ago. That kingdom was about 750 years old at the time of the American Revolution. Among the great men of that old Poland was the astronomer, Copernicus. Very soon after the American Revolution, Poland's armies were defeated by

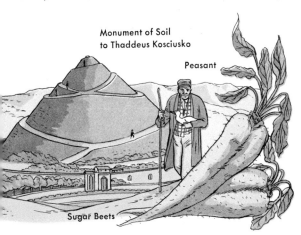

Monument of Soil
to Thaddeus Kosciusko

Peasant

Sugar Beets

armies of powerful neighbors, and the old Poland was divided among those neighbors.

A new Poland was not born till 1919, at the end of World War I. It was an independent republic. It was only 20 years old when World War II brought great destruction to it. That war brought changes in the new Poland's boundaries, too. Part of what was eastern Poland now belongs to the Soviet Union. But from Germany Poland gained much Baltic coast and the westernmost part of what today is Poland's rich southwestern industrial region.

Most of Warsaw's buildings are new. They stand on recent ruins of the city. In Cracow, many buildings are centuries old. Near Cracow is a monument to Kosciusko, a Polish general who helped Americans win the American Revolution.

The Polish people have suffered many hardships since World War II. But conditions seem to have improved somewhat since 1956. Wages have increased a little. Some rules are not so strict. It is hoped that better times for the Polish people are ahead. (See COPERNICUS; WORLD WAR I; WORLD WAR II.)

POLIOMYELITIS (po li o my e LY tis) This disease is usually called polio. It is chiefly a children's disease, but grownups may have it, too. Polio can kill, and it leaves many people crippled.

Polio is caused by a kind of disease germ called a virus. It is thought that the polio virus is spread from one person to another, but no one is sure just how. When the polio virus gets into a person's body, it may attack the nerve cells that control muscles. If it damages or destroys the nerve cells, the muscles will not be able to work properly.

For years no one knew how to prevent polio. Then, in 1955, Dr. Jonas Salk developed a polio vaccine. Three shots of this vaccine taken at intervals protect most people. Soon polio may be as rare as smallpox. (See IRON LUNG.)

Each political party holds a convention to choose its candidates.

POLITICAL PARTIES In many countries today the people govern themselves. Each of these countries can have what the majority of its people want in the way of such things as laws and services. But there has to be some political machinery for letting people go about getting what they want. Political parties are an important part of this machinery.

A political party is made up of people who have more or less the same ideas about what should be done. At the time of an election each political party chooses candidates who will try to carry out the wishes of the party. The voters are then able to vote for these candidates.

Political parties change. A party may break up because there are too many disagreements among its members. Or a question for which one party stood may be settled for good and all so that there is no longer any need for the party. When one party disappears, another party is very likely to be formed.

In the United States today there are two strong political parties — the Democratic party and the Republican party. Besides these two there are other parties that have fewer members.

It is important that a country have at least two parties. If there is only one party, voting does not mean anything. In Germany, from 1933 until he died at the end of World War II, Hitler pretended that the people were ruling themselves. But the only political party was the Nazi party.

On the other hand, it becomes hard for a majority of the people in a country to get the kind of government they want if there are a great many political parties, none very strong. Germany was a republic for a time after World War I. But the republic failed partly because the people were divided up among too many political parties. No matter what party won an election, a very large number of the people were dissatisfied. Things might have been very different if some of the parties could have buried their less important disagreements and joined together. France is another country that has had rough sailing because of too many political parties.

In the United States political parties are most important at the time of a presidential election. Then each party has a big convention at which it chooses its candidates. At the convention, too, the party writes its platform. A party platform is a list of things the party will work for if its candidates are elected. Now the people of the United States have a very good idea of what these conventions are like, for they can see them on television. They can see their machinery of government working. (See DEMOCRACY; GOVERNMENT; NAZIS; UNITED STATES GOVERNMENT.)

Insects in Clover

Bumblebee

Sweat Bee

POLLINATION Peach blossoms have four kinds of parts: sepals, petals, stamens, and pistils. The stamens produce pollen. The pistils contain ovules, the beginnings of seeds. Before a peach ovule is able to become a seed, however, a grain of peach pollen must reach the top of the pistil and grow down to the ovule.

The story of other seeds is much the same. No flowers can produce seeds unless pollen reaches their pistils. The transfer of pollen grains from stamens to pistils is called pollination.

In some cases the pollen from the stamens of a flower simply falls on the pistil of the same flower. This kind of pollination is called self-pollination. But in a great many cases self-pollination does not work. No seeds are formed. The pollen must come from another flower.

Clearly, most pollen must go traveling. Some of it rides on the wind. Some rides on the bodies of insects.

Insects carry pollen as they go from flower to flower to get food. Bees are by far the most important insect pollen carriers. The perfume and color of many flowers help to attract insects.

A plant may depend on one certain kind of insect to carry its pollen. Only hawk moths can pollinate the hawk moth orchid. Red clover depends mostly on bumblebees. A shortage of bumblebees means a poor crop of clover seed.

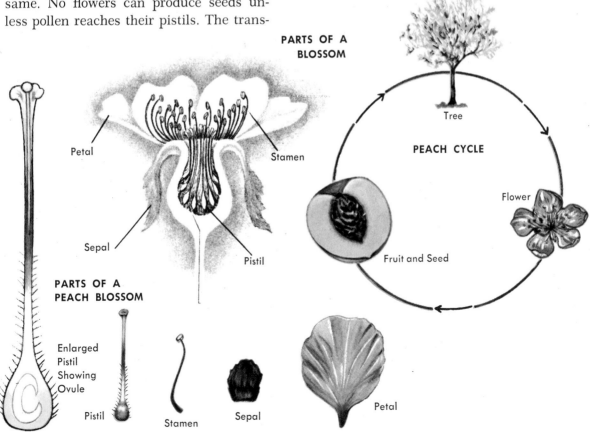

PARTS OF A BLOSSOM

Petal

Stamen

Sepal

Pistil

PARTS OF A PEACH BLOSSOM

Enlarged Pistil Showing Ovule

Pistil

Stamen

Sepal

Petal

Tree

PEACH CYCLE

Flower

Fruit and Seed

From horses, polo players hit the ball toward the goal.

POLO The game of polo is very much like hockey except that it is played on horseback. The rider hits a white ball with a mallet and tries to drive it between two goal posts. The mallet he uses is like a croquet mallet with a long handle that bends easily. But the player usually hits the ball with the side of the mallet, not with one end as in croquet.

Every polo game is divided into parts called chukkers. A chukker is seven and one-half minutes long. A game may be made up of six, seven, or eight chukkers with short periods between them.

Polo is one of the fastest of all games. The players on their ponies dash madly from one end of the field to the other. A polo pony has to be able to start and stop very quickly. It has to keep its eyes on the ball. No player can play a good game unless he is riding a good pony. For every game he needs at least two ponies, and he often uses more. He changes ponies after every chukker. Sometimes a player's pony kicks the ball between the goal posts. A goal made in this way is called a pony goal.

Polo is played both indoors and outdoors. Of course, it can be played indoors only in a big field house of some kind. When polo is played outdoors there are four players on each side. When it is played indoors there are only three.

Many more people would like to play polo than can. It costs too much for most people. A good polo pony may cost several thousand dollars. It takes a great deal of time and patience to train one. Of course, a player must see that his ponies are well cared for, too.

Polo is a very old game. It was being played in Persia at least 2,000 years ago. It reached England by way of India in the 1800's. Now the countries where polo is played most often are India, England, Argentina, and the United States. Often there are matches that bring teams from all these countries together. A good polo match is great fun to see. (See HOCKEY.)

POMPEII In the year 79, three small Roman cities were buried in an eruption of the volcano Vesuvius. One of the three cities was Pompeii.

Pompeii lay on the shores of the Bay of Naples, only a mile from the foot of Vesuvius. It was a prosperous little city, and many of its people were rich. The city boasted seven temples, two theaters, three public baths, a great amphitheater, and a big open market place. Its streets were paved, and its houses were mostly two-storied. Beautiful statues and paintings were to be found in the houses. A wall with eight gateways surrounded the city.

The people of Pompeii were not afraid of Vesuvius. It had been quiet for at least 700 years, and they did not dream that it would ever erupt again. The last lava that had poured from the volcano had been broken up into rich soil on the lower slopes of the mountain. Many of the people of Pompeii had vineyards on those slopes.

On August 24 of the year 79 the Pompeians found out how mistaken they had been. A rain of pellets of pumice fell on the city as the famous eruption began. Soon the streets were deep in pumice. Of course, the people—at least most of them—tried to escape. About 18,000 of the 20,000 who lived there got away.

For hour after hour the pumice continued to fall. At last the rain of pumice stopped and a rain of fine volcanic ash began. When the three-day eruption ended,

Pompeii was deeply buried. And the shore line had been changed so much that no one could tell exactly where Pompeii had been.

The city was hidden for nearly 17 centuries. In 1748 a farmer digging in his vineyard near the foot of the mountain came across traces of the buried city. He told about his find. Scholars saw that from the buried city they might be able to find out a great deal about the lives of the ancient Romans. Digging began, and little by little the city was uncovered. More than half of the excavating has now been done. Travelers today go by the thousands to see the resurrected city.

Mt. Vesuvius and the Ruins of Pompeii   *Joe Barnell-Shostal*

The roofs of the buildings are gone, but the walls, in part, are still standing. Ovens, cooking pans, wax tablets, bathtubs, marble tables, and bronze statues help tell the story of how the people of Pompeii lived. There can even be seen the ruts in the paving stones made by Roman chariots, and the stepping stones the people used in crossing the streets.

Very little jewelry has been found. The Pompeians when they fled must have carried most of their jewelry with them.

When the workmen were digging down through the rocky layers of ashes and pumice, one of them noticed a queer-shaped cavity. He knew that it must have been made by something which had been buried in the eruption and had then disappeared. He poured concrete into the cavity. When it had hardened, he dug away the rock around it and found that he had a perfect cast of a dog. After it was buried by the ashes and pumice, the dog's body had gradually changed to dust.

Ruins of the Law Courts   *Rupert Leach-Shostal*

In the same way the workmen made casts of people who had lost their lives as they were trying to escape. They found, it is said, one sentry who had apparently refused to leave his post. The sentry did not guess that people would learn about his bravery 17 centuries later! (See ARCHEOLOGY; ROADS AND STREETS; ROME, ANCIENT; VESUVIUS; VOLCANOES.)

Fresco on Wall of Villa   *Philip D. Gendreau*

Pony Express riders carried the western mail.

PONY EXPRESS Before 1860 there was no quick way of getting mail from the eastern half of the United States to the Far West. There were no railroads across the Great Plains. Of course there were no automobiles or airplanes. The fastest way to send mail was by stagecoach. That was not very fast. It usually took at least 25 days to travel the 2,000 miles from the Mississippi River to the west coast.

In 1860 a plan was made to send mail by "pony express." Riders with fast horses were to be stationed along the route and the mail was to be passed from one rider to the next. Each trip was to be like a relay race. The pony express would run between Sacramento, Calif., and St. Joseph, Mo.

The plan was pushed ahead fast. Stations were built along the route. In regions where the Indians were not friendly the stations were little fortresses.

The best horses that could be had were bought. Each one was expected to cover ten to twenty miles at top speed over roads that were often very bad.

The riders were all young. They were chosen for their light weight, their bravery, and their general fitness. Everyone knew that the life of a pony express rider would be full of hardship, danger, and thrilling adventure.

April 3 was the day set for the pony express to begin. In San Francisco a pony stood waiting with a load of mail. Two little flags decorated his bridle, and from his saddle hung a bag labeled "Overland Pony Express." When the signal was given, the pony and his rider boarded the boat that was to carry them to Sacramento. There the real pony express began. William Hamilton, the first rider, started eastward. He covered the first 57 miles half an hour ahead of schedule.

On the same day Billy Richardson in St. Joseph waited for the westbound mail to reach his station. He wore a buckskin jacket and a red flannel shirt. His riding boots were of the finest leather. The train bringing in the mail was late. But at last, just before dark, a cannon roared to announce that the mail had arrived. The young rider jumped on his horse and was off as the crowds shouted.

There were big celebrations when the mail reached the ends of the line. The going had not been easy. In some places in the mountains the riders had found 30 feet of snow. But they had made the trip much faster than the bulky stagecoaches had ever made it.

The riders carried the mail in small leather bags. These were sewn to a square of leather that fitted over the saddle. One bag was in front and one behind each leg of the rider. The letters, before they were put in the bags, were wrapped in oiled silk to keep them dry. At each stop two minutes were allowed for changing the mail bags to a fresh pony. At first each rider rode from 30 to 50 miles. Soon the run was lengthened to from 75 to 100 miles.

The riders had many encounters with the Indians. One night, for instance, a rider saw an Indian campfire ahead. There was no way of avoiding it. When he came close, he began firing his pistol and shouting. The Indians thought that a big party of white men had come to attack them. They fled. Later the rider heard that the Indians had planned to catch him to find out how the express riders went so fast.

Even the ponies acted as if they knew that their work was very important. One time after a rider had been killed and scalped by Indians, the pony broke away from the band of Indians and carried the mail safely to the next station.

The danger from Indians was only one of the many dangers the riders had to face. Bandits often held up the pony express just as they held up stagecoaches. Bad weather was a great danger, too.

One of the most important trips ever made by pony express was made in the fall of 1860. It carried the news that Abraham Lincoln had been elected president. By this time telegraph lines had been built as far west as St. Joseph. They had been built eastward from California as far as Fort Churchill, Nev. The pony express carried the news the 1,800 miles from St. Joseph to Fort Churchill. Then it was telegraphed to San Francisco.

By October of 1861 the telegraph line from the East met the one from the West. Then the pony express came to an end. "The pony was fast," someone wrote, "but he could not compete with the lightning." (See U.S. POSTAL SERVICE.)

Porcupine Footprints   Porcupine Raising Quills at Enemy

PORCUPINE The porcupine is one of the gnawing animals, or rodents. It is, therefore, a cousin of the mouse, rat, and squirrel, although it does not look at all like any one of them. It is much larger—a full-grown porcupine is about a yard long. Besides, it is covered with quills. Porcupines are sometimes called "quill pigs." They are sometimes called "hedgehogs," too, but they should not be, for in Europe and western Asia there is a true hedgehog which is not a rodent.

The story that porcupines throw their quills is not true. They cannot throw their

The porcupine eats wood and inner bark.

quills, but the quills do come out easily. With one swift swish of its quill-covered tail a porcupine can make an animal that attacks it howl with pain. A porcupine's quills are several inches long and are barbed like fishhooks at the ends. If a porcupine quill gets a firm hold in the skin of another animal, it is very hard to pull out. Few animals dare attack a porcupine.

American porcupines are good tree climbers. They eat chiefly leaves, twigs, bark, and wood. They sometimes visit camps and eat shovel handles and leather boots. They will nibble on anything salty. American porcupines are good swimmers, but are slow and clumsy on the ground.

Baby porcupines are born in late spring. Their home is usually in a hollow log but is sometimes in cracks among the rocks.

Porcupine meat is good to eat. Laws have been made to help protect porcupines.

All porcupines have quills and are plant-eaters, but some of those in other lands are quite different from the American porcupines. Those of South America have long, thin tails that they can use in holding on to branches of the trees they live in. The porcupines of Europe, Asia, and Africa dig their homes in the ground and cannot climb trees. (See RODENTS.)

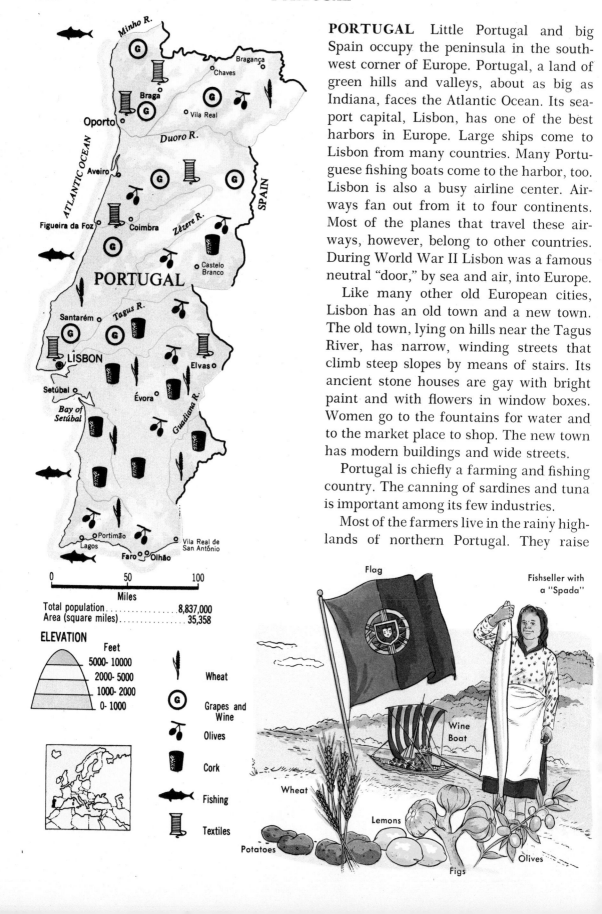

PORTUGAL Little Portugal and big Spain occupy the peninsula in the southwest corner of Europe. Portugal, a land of green hills and valleys, about as big as Indiana, faces the Atlantic Ocean. Its seaport capital, Lisbon, has one of the best harbors in Europe. Large ships come to Lisbon from many countries. Many Portuguese fishing boats come to the harbor, too. Lisbon is also a busy airline center. Airways fan out from it to four continents. Most of the planes that travel these airways, however, belong to other countries. During World War II Lisbon was a famous neutral "door," by sea and air, into Europe.

Like many other old European cities, Lisbon has an old town and a new town. The old town, lying on hills near the Tagus River, has narrow, winding streets that climb steep slopes by means of stairs. Its ancient stone houses are gay with bright paint and with flowers in window boxes. Women go to the fountains for water and to the market place to shop. The new town has modern buildings and wide streets.

Portugal is chiefly a farming and fishing country. The canning of sardines and tuna is important among its few industries.

Most of the farmers live in the rainy highlands of northern Portugal. They raise

Total population 8,837,000
Area (square miles) 35,358

ELEVATION

Feet
5000- 10000
2000- 5000
1000- 2000
0- 1000

Wheat

Grapes and Wine

Olives

Cork

Fishing

Textiles

Flag

Fishseller with a "Spada"

Wine Boat

Wheat

Lemons

Potatoes

Figs

Olives

Potatoes

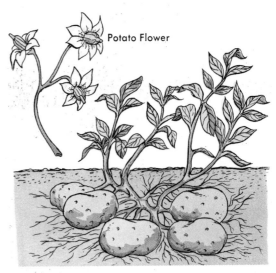
Potato Flower

Potatoes form below the ground.

many kinds of grain, which they feed to livestock, including bulls for bullfights. In the valleys of the Tagus and Douro rivers farmers tend vineyards. On the hillsides are thriving olive orchards. Warm southern Portugal is fruit country. In February travelers come to see the sweet-almond orchards in masses of pink bloom.

Portugal has great forests of cork oak on its mountainsides. Many Portuguese workers cut and sell cork from the oak trees.

The Portuguese carry on some trade with their colonies, Angola and Mozambique, in Africa, and with the nearby Portuguese islands, the Azores and Madeiras. The Portuguese trade with other countries, too, buying chiefly manufactured goods.

Few big ships carry the flag of Portugal. But the world remembers that 500 years ago the Portuguese Prince Henry, the Navigator, set up a naval school on the coast, hired the best map makers and the most daring sailors, and sent out ships of exploration. Portuguese seamen were the first to reach India by sailing around southern Africa. They were the first to reach Brazil, in South America. Explorers helped Portugal to build an empire. (See BRAZIL; CORK; EUROPE; EXPLORERS; OLIVES; PENINSULA; SOUTH AMERICA; SPAIN.)

POTATO The Irish potato—our common white potato — is sometimes called the world's No. 1 vegetable. It is almost without question the most important vegetable of Europe and the Americas.

In spite of its name, the Irish potato did not come first from Ireland. It came instead from the mountains of South America. There are still wild potatoes to be found growing in the mountains of Peru and several other South American countries.

The potato was first taken from South America to other parts of the world soon after the Spanish explorer Pizarro conquered Peru. Pizarro was hunting for gold and other such riches. He did not guess that the new vegetable he had found was going to be worth much more to the world than the boatloads of gold and silver he carried away with him.

For some reason—no one knows exactly why—the potato came to be an important vegetable in Ireland before it became important in any of the other countries in Europe. In this way it got the "Irish" in its name. It was brought to New England from Ireland in 1719.

The part of the potato we eat is an underground stem. It grows big because the potato plant stores up a great deal of food in it. When the potato was first taken to Germany, the Germans did not understand what part of the plant they were to eat. They ate the bitter seed pods and decided that the potato was not a good vegetable. When they found out their mistake, potatoes became very popular.

Tons of potatoes are raised every year in the United States. Some states are famous for their potatoes. One is Idaho. Another is Maine. (See IDAHO; MAINE; PERU; VEGETABLES.)

Older baby opossums travel on their mothers' backs.

Newborn
Opossums
in Spoon

POUCHED MAMMALS Kangaroos carry their babies in pouches. When a baby kangaroo is born, it is not any bigger than a child's little finger. A kangaroo baby has no fur, and it is blind and helpless. The baby at once crawls into its mother's pouch. There it gets milk, for kangaroos are mammals. All mammals feed their babies with milk from their bodies.

A number of other mammals have pouches. Only one group of pouched mammals lives in the Americas. They are the opossums. All the other pouched mammals live in Australia or on islands near by.

The babies of all the pouched mammals are tiny and helpless when they are born. They could not live if they did not have a warm, safe place to stay in.

The plan of carrying their babies in pouches is a very old plan among the mammals. There were pouched mammals long before there were horses or rabbits or whales. In most parts of the world the pouched mammals have been crowded out. They have been crowded out by mammals that carry their babies inside their bodies long enough so that the babies do not need pouches after they are born.

Pouched mammals have another name. This other name is marsupials. (See AUSTRALIA; BANDICOOT; KANGAROO; KOALA; MAMMALS; WOMBAT.)

The kangaroo, a native of Australia, carries its young in a stomach pouch.

VARIETIES OF CHICKENS

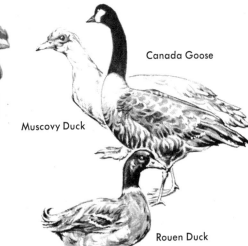

Canada Goose

Muscovy Duck

Rouen Duck

POULTRY We get all our eggs and part of our meat from birds we have tamed. The birds we raise to furnish us with food are called domestic fowl, or poultry. Chickens, turkeys, ducks, and geese are poultry. So are pigeons and guinea fowl. In a year Americans eat on the average nearly 20 pounds of poultry apiece.

Chickens furnish almost all our eggs. Not many people eat eggs of any other kind. Chickens furnish a great deal of meat, too. There are many breeds of chickens. They differ in color and size and shape and in the shape of their combs. Some breeds of chickens are better for meat. Others are better for laying eggs.

Turkeys are larger than chickens. Next to chickens they are the most popular of our fowls. Ducks come next, and then geese. Geese are raised for their feathers as well as for their meat. Goose down is used to stuff pillows. In early days large goose feathers, or quills, were used as pens. Pigeons are much smaller than chickens. Most of those eaten are eaten when they are young. Young pigeons are called squabs.

Bronze Turkey

Guinea fowl are not at all common. Most people have never tasted one.

In America most of the poultry and eggs eaten come from special poultry farms. But nearly every farm has at least a small flock of chickens. (See DOMESTICATED ANIMALS; PIGEONS; TURKEY.)

PRAIRIE The early settlers along the eastern shores of the United States had to clear forests away to get homes for themselves. When they pushed westward, they found forest land for hundreds of miles. But then they came to great stretches of flat grassland. The grass was so tall that it reached to the knees of their horses. These grasslands are called prairies.

Prairies covered most of Illinois, Indiana, Wisconsin, Missouri, and Iowa. So much of Illinois was prairie that it was nicknamed the Prairie State. Parts of Ohio and Minnesota were prairie, too.

At first the settlers did not want to build homes on the prairies. They thought that there were no trees because the land was poor. Later they found that they were wrong. Prairie soil is rich soil.

There are prairies in other parts of the Americas, too. There are three prairie provinces in Canada. One of the prairies of South America is the vast one in Argentina called the Pampa. (See ARGENTINA; PIONEER LIFE IN AMERICA.)

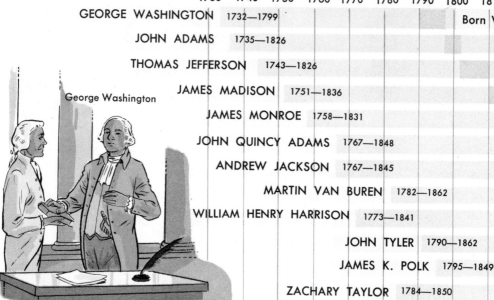

George Washington

	1730	1740	1750	1760	1770	1780	1790	1800	1810	1820	18
GEORGE WASHINGTON	1732—1799							Born Virginia—Fed
JOHN ADAMS	1735—1826						
THOMAS JEFFERSON		1743—1826				
JAMES MADISON		1751—1836				
JAMES MONROE			1758—1831			
JOHN QUINCY ADAMS			1767—1848			
ANDREW JACKSON			1767—1845			
MARTIN VAN BUREN				1782—1862		
WILLIAM HENRY HARRISON				1773—1841		
JOHN TYLER				1790—1862		
JAMES K. POLK				1795—1849		
ZACHARY TAYLOR				1784—1850		
MILLARD FILLMORE					1800—1874	
FRANKLIN PIERCE					1804—1869	
JAMES BUCHANAN				1791—1868		
ABRAHAM LINCOLN					1809—1865	
ANDREW JOHNSON					1808—1875	
ULYSSES S. GRANT						1822—
RUTHERFORD B. HAYES						1822—
JAMES A. GARFIELD						
CHESTER A. ARTHUR						
GROVER CLEVELAND						
BENJAMIN HARRISON						
WILLIAM McKINLEY						
THEODORE ROOSE						
WILLIAM HOWARD						
WOODROW WIL						
WARREN G. HARD						
CALVIN COOL						
HERBERT HOO						
FRANKLIN D. ROOSE						

PRESIDENTS OF THE UNITED STATES Every four years the people of the United States elect a president. The election is held on the first Tuesday after the first Monday in November. The president who is elected begins his term at noon on the next January 20.

No one can be elected president unless he was born in the United States and has lived in the country for 14 years. No one, moreover, can be elected president unless he is at least 35 years old.

If a president dies, the vice-president becomes president. Several vice-presidents who became president in this way were themselves later elected president.

Until 1951 there was no law telling how many times a man could be president. But no one before Franklin D. Roosevelt had ever been elected more than twice. He was elected four times. In 1951 the rule was made that no future president could be elected more than twice.

Was Franklin D. Roosevelt the 31st president or the 32nd? People do not agree about the right answer. For no one is sure whether to count Grover Cleveland once or twice. He was elected president in 1884. He was defeated in 1888 but was elected again in 1892.

860 1870 1880 1890 1900 1910 1920 1930 1940 1950 1960

chusetts—Federalist

ia—Democrat-Republican

Virginia—Democrat-Republican

Virginia—Democrat-Republican

Massachusetts—Democrat-Republican

South Carolina—Democrat

Born New York—Democrat

Virginia—Whig

Born Virginia—Whig

North Carolina—Democrat

n Virginia—Whig

Born New York—Whig

Born New Hampshire—Democrat

Born Pennsylvania—Democrat

Born Kentucky—Republican

Born North Carolina—Democrat

Born Ohio—Republican

Born Ohio—Republican

Born Ohio—Republican

Born Vermont—Republican

—1908   Born New Jersey—Democrat

—1901   Born Ohio—Republican

—1901   Born Ohio—Republican

1858—1919   Born New York—Republican

1857—1930   Born Ohio—Republican

1856—1924   Born Virginia—Democrat

1865—1923   Born Ohio—Republican

1872—1933   Born Vermont—Republican

1874—   Born Iowa—Republican

1882—1945   Born New York—Democrat

RRY S. TRUMAN 1884—   Born Missouri—Democrat

GHT D. EISENHOWER 1890—   Born Texas—Republican

Thomas Jefferson

James Monroe

Abraham Lincoln

Theodore Roosevelt

Franklin Roosevelt

Oxygen made the mouse more active.

PRIESTLEY, JOSEPH (1733-1804) Almost every school child knows that the air around us contains oxygen. Everybody needs oxygen to remain alive. Oxygen is by far the most abundant chemical element on earth. Yet, strangely enough, no one knew anything about oxygen until Joseph Priestley discovered it on August 1, 1774—less than 200 years ago.

Priestley discovered oxygen while heating red oxide of mercury—a chemical which contains oxygen. Oxygen escapes as a gas when the chemical is heated. Priestley filled a jar with the gas and put a mouse into it. The mouse became very active. Priestley burned a candle in the gas and found that it burned more brightly than it did in air. He breathed some of the gas and it made him feel very energetic.

At this time all gases were called "airs." Priestley called this gas which he had discovered the "perfect air," probably because it did such wonderful things.

Although Priestley saw that things burn more brightly in oxygen than in air, he did not realize that it is oxygen that makes things burn. But his discovery led to a true explanation of burning 20 years later by the French scientist Lavoisier (la vwa zee AY). Lavoisier named the gas.

Priestley had not planned to be a scientist. He was really a minister. Doing chemical experiments, especially with "airs," was his hobby. He discovered several other gases besides oxygen. Among them was laughing gas, which is sometimes used as an anesthetic by dentists. He also invented laboratory equipment for collecting gases. His hobby made him famous.

Priestley was born in England and lived most of his life there. But he did much traveling and lived for some time in Paris, where he became a friend of Lavoisier. Priestley came to be greatly disliked in his homeland because of some of the ideas he preached. His life was even in danger. In 1794 he moved to America. He made his home in America until his death in 1804. (See AIR; ANESTHETICS; CHEMISTRY; ELEMENTS; FIRE; OXYGEN.)

PRINTING   When people talk about printing, they usually mean printing with separate type letters. Printing of a kind had been known for centuries before printing with separate letters was invented. Every time, for instance, a Babylonian signed a document by rolling his "cylinder seal" on the wet clay tablet the document was written on, he was really printing.

The oldest printed book known was made in China in 848 by Wang Chieh. He planned it to honor his parents. Each page was first carved by hand on a block of wood. The block was then inked and a sheet of paper was pressed down on it. The separate pages were then pasted together.

The idea of printing with wood blocks spread to Europe. The letters in block books were made to look like handwritten letters. The first letters of a paragraph were often colored by hand.

As early as Roman times children had alphabet blocks. But it was a long, long time before anyone had the idea of printing with separate letters fastened together to make words and sentences. The Chinese, it is thought, first had the idea of printing

Chinese Block Print

Enlarged Cylinder Seal

Babylonian Using Cylinder Seal

in this way. They are believed to have printed with porcelain type about 900 years ago. But not much came of their invention. The idea of separate letter type—movable type, it is called—did not spread from China to Europe.

Printing with movable type was invented in Europe about five centuries ago. No one is sure who invented it. Johann Gutenberg, who lived in Mainz, Germany, is usually given the credit. He was certainly one of the earliest printers to use movable type.

Why didn't the inventor of printing announce his great discovery? Probably because he did not want anyone to know that his books were not done by hand. In those days people thought that everything was better if it was done by hand.

A difficult part of an early printer's work was making the many letters that were needed. To set up in type a page like this one, for instance, would take 292 *e*'s. Early type-making was a great deal like casting lead soldiers. Lead was melted and poured into molds. Of course it was not easy to make good molds. Gutenberg, however, made excellent ones.

A printer kept his type in cases made up of many little compartments. There was a separate compartment for each letter. When a printer wanted to print a page,

he first had to choose the letters he needed and put them in place. He used a frame that would hold them in the right position. When a page had been set, the printer put it in the proper position on his printing press and inked it.

Early printing presses were run by hand. The printer, after inking his type, put a piece of damp paper down on it. To make each letter print clearly, the paper had to be pressed down on the type. The printer pressed the paper down against the type by covering the type and paper with a wooden slab and then screwing it down by turning a big screw. It took a strong back to turn the screw of a press. After a printer had made as many copies of a page as he wished, he cleaned the type and put all the letters back into their compartments.

For more than 300 years printing did not change much. People got over their feeling against it, and print shops sprang up in many places. But all the shops were much like the early shops. True, presses came to be made of iron instead of wood. But otherwise there was little change.

The steam engine, when it came into use, brought about a great change in printing. Presses were built that could be run by steam engines. These presses were very much better than the early presses. They

Early American Press

speeded up printing tremendously. In fact, printing was speeded up so much that something had to be done to speed up typesetting. Many men tried to invent a machine that would take type from a case and set it in lines of the proper length, but all of them failed.

At last an American thought of a way of solving the problem. His name was Ottmar Mergenthaler. He invented a machine that would cast a whole line of type at one time. His machine was called a Linotype. Another American, Tolbert Lanston, invented a machine that cast one letter at a time and set it in place—a Monotype machine.

A casting machine can cast more than 100 letters a minute. This paragraph could be set in type in less than a minute.

The metal that is used in casting type has to be metal that can be melted without too much heat. It has to be "soft." Usually it is made mostly of lead. Letters made of such soft metal wear down if they are used many times. If a page of type is to be used for printing a great many copies, electricity is used to make a copy of the page in copper and nickel. The copper-nickel copy is thin. Soft type metal is put on the back to make it strong. This new page of type can then be put on the press.

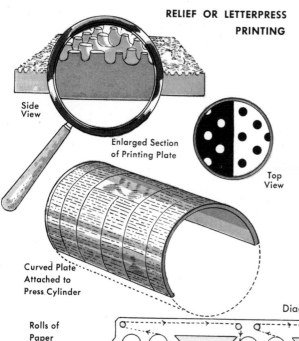

RELIEF OR LETTERPRESS PRINTING

Side View

Enlarged Section of Printing Plate

Top View

Curved Plate Attached to Press Cylinder

Diagram of a "Perfecting" Press

Rolls of Paper

Folded Sections Ready for Binding

The diagram of a "perfecting" press (above) shows how four colors are printed on first one side of a moving sheet of paper and then on the other.

Pressman

Folder

Pressman

Pressman

Eight-color, Roll-fed, Perfecting Press

Any kind of printing in which paper is pressed against raised type is called letterpress. Letterpress is the kind of printing that was done in the very early days of printing, and most of the presses of today still use the same process.

This book was printed on one of the most modern presses in the world by a process that is very different from letterpress. The process is called offset lithography, or offset printing. An entirely different type of printing plate is used in offset printing. This plate never touches the paper on which the printing is done.

The first steps in printing this book were to set type by linotype and to have artists draw and color the illustrations. The type was used to make one print, or proof. This was photographed. The illustrations were photographed, too. The negatives of the type and of the illustrations were rephotographed on thin metal plates treated with photographic chemicals. On these metal plates the pictures of the type and the illustrations were formed by a thin film of the chemicals.

Printing from plates of this sort is possible because oil and water will not mix. Inks like those used in printing this book contain oil. They will stick to the part of a

A four-color, sheet-fed, offset lithographic press delivers sheets that are fully printed on one side. The sheets must be put through the press a second time to print the other side.

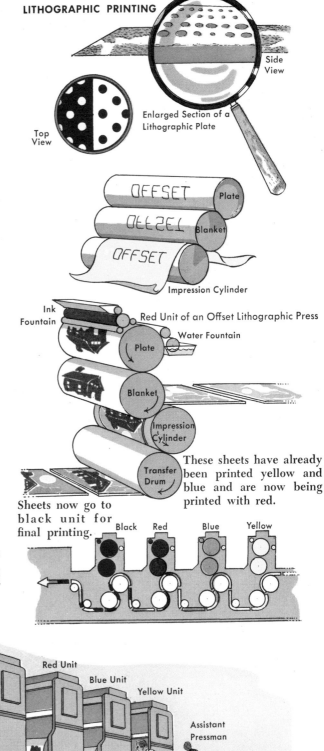

LITHOGRAPHIC PRINTING

Side View

Enlarged Section of a Lithographic Plate

Top View

OFFSET

Plate

Blanket

Impression Cylinder

Ink Fountain

Red Unit of an Offset Lithographic Press

Water Fountain

Plate

Blanket

Impression Cylinder

Transfer Drum

These sheets have already been printed yellow and blue and are now being printed with red.

Sheets now go to black unit for final printing.

Black   Red   Blue   Yellow

Black Unit

Red Unit

Blue Unit

Yellow Unit

Assistant Pressman

Feeding End

Printed Sheets

Pressman

Diagram of Four-color, Sheet-fed, Offset Lithographic Press

This picture was made with four separate plates—red, yellow, blue, and black.

plate that has the chemical film on it. They will not stick to the rest of the plate because that part of the plate is kept wet with water during the printing process.

As the press that printed this book was running, each printing plate pressed against a rubber roller. Ink that was on the plate was transferred to the rubber roller. This roller then pressed against the printing paper and the ink went onto the paper.

In order to print black-and-white photographs by either letterpress or offset, the photograph has to be broken up into dots. Look through a magnifying glass at any black-and-white photograph in a book or newspaper and you will see that it is a dot picture. The black dots are largest where the picture is darkest. They are smallest where the picture is lightest.

All colored pictures, whether printed by letterpress or offset, are dot pictures, too. The dots in colored pictures, as one would know, are not all black. Some of the dots in the pictures in this book are red, some are yellow, and some are blue. Colored pictures like these are much more expensive than black-and-white pictures because four different plates have to be made for each picture. One plate prints only the red dots, one only the black dots, one only the blue dots, and one only the yellow dots.

In addition to letterpress and offset, there are still other methods of printing. Intaglio (in TAL yo), which is just the reverse of letterpress, has the printing design cut into the surface of the printing plate. Rotogravure is actually intaglio printing. Silk screen printing is often used for printing on glass or metal. Mimeograph and Multigraph machines are small office printing devices.

The past 500 years have seen many great inventions. Some people call printing the greatest of them all. (See ALPHABET; BOOKS AND BOOKBINDING.)

Magnified
Section of
Picture
Showing Dots

PROTECTIVE COLORING

A katydid is safer because its color is green, a horned toad is safer because it is brown, and a polar bear is safer because it is white. Each is safer because its color is so much the same as the color of the place where it lives. The katydid with its wings folded is so much like a droopy green leaf that its enemies are not likely to see it. A horned toad flattens its grayish-brown body on the grayish-brown sand and is hard to see, too. A polar bear covers its black nose with its paws, curls up on the snow, and looks like more snow. If an animal's color helps it hide, we say that the animal has protective coloring. Or we may say that it is well camouflaged. Good camouflage is very common in the animal world.

In regions of warm summers and cold winters some animals change their dress with the seasons. In the winter weasels, for instance, have white fur that matches the snow. In the summer they are brown and not easily seen in woods and fields.

Some animals actually change color as their surroundings change. The common tree toad is a good example. If it is resting on a leaf, it is green. If it is on bark, it is either gray or brown.

The pattern the colors of an animal form may be as important as the colors themselves. Stripes and spots may make an animal's coat match the usual forest pattern of sunlight and shadow. They may keep the outline of the animal from showing

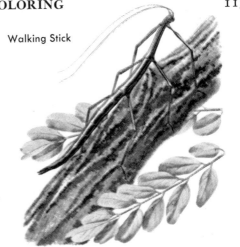

Walking Stick

clearly. The tiger, leopard, giraffe, and sargassum fish are among the animals with spots or stripes that help them match their natural surroundings.

As in the case of the katydid, shape may go hand in hand with color in helping an animal hide. A walking stick on a twig may go unseen partly because it is brown like the twig but also because it has the shape of a twig. A tree hopper is hard to tell from a thorn because it is both the color and the shape of a thorn.

An animal's protective coloring does not help much unless the animal stays quiet. A toad looks like a clump of dirt in the garden only as long as it does not start hopping. Rabbits and some other animals are said to "freeze" because they stay so very quiet when an enemy is near. (See ADAPTATION TO ENVIRONMENT; CAMOUFLAGE; SLOTH.)

As winter approaches, the weasel's coat starts turning white.

PROTESTANT CHURCHES For 1,500 years all Christians worshiped Christ in much the same way. They were all Catholics. The Christians of western Europe made up the Roman Catholic Church. The head of this church was the pope.

The word "protestant" comes from "protest." In the 1500's some of the Christians in western Europe wanted to change some of the practices of the church. They had their own ideas of how God should be worshiped. They declared, or protested, their ideas. Martin Luther was the first great leader of the protesters. John Calvin came soon afterward. Their churches came to be called Protestant churches.

Since the time of these two early leaders, one group after another has broken away from the Catholic Church and from the early Protestant groups. Now there are a great many Protestant churches. They are often called denominations. Calling them denominations keeps them from being confused with the buildings, or churches, where their followers worship.

Services in most Protestant churches are quite different from Catholic services. For one thing, the people in the congregations take a greater part in the services. As a rule, the services are much simpler than in Catholic churches.

The list below names twelve of the leading Protestant denominations. It tells in round numbers how many people in the United States belong to each one, and how many church buildings in the United States each one has.

Denomination	Churches	Members
Baptist	89,500	19,766,000
Churches of Christ	16,500	1,750,000
Church of Christ, Scientist	2,350	
Congregational	5,550	1,393,000
Disciples of Christ	8,000	1,944,000
Friends (Quakers)	985	120,000
Latter-day Saints (Mormons)	3,900	1,491,000
Lutheran	16,780	7,530,000
Methodist	54,000	12,059,000
Presbyterian	14,550	4,043,000
Protestant Episcopal	6,840	2,965,000
Unitarian	365	105,000

(See CHRISTIANITY; QUAKERS; RELIGIONS OF THE WORLD; ROMAN CATHOLIC CHURCH.)

Church of Christ the King
Seattle, Washington

Riverside Church
New York City,
New York

Hopewell Baptist Church
Edmond, Oklahoma

Old North Church
Boston, Massachusetts

Congregational Church
Kent, Connecticut

Congregational Church
Farmington, Connecticut

Old Brick Church
Smithfield, Virginia

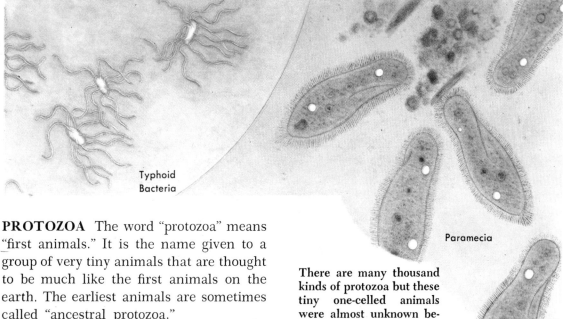

Typhoid Bacteria

Paramecia

PROTOZOA The word "protozoa" means "first animals." It is the name given to a group of very tiny animals that are thought to be much like the first animals on the earth. The earliest animals are sometimes called "ancestral protozoa."

Until microscopes were invented we knew almost nothing about such tiny animals. Without a microscope the very largest protozoa look like tiny specks. The giants among them measure only about a tenth of an inch. Most kinds of protozoa cannot be seen at all with the naked eye.

These tiny animals have only one cell in their bodies. But this one-celled body can carry on all sorts of activities. It can digest food, get rid of its waste, breathe, and produce more like itself.

Protozoa are found all over the world in both fresh water and salt water. If we put a drop of pond water under a microscope we are almost sure to see several of these tiny animals moving about. They are also found inside the bodies of other animals. They get food from the bodies of the animals they live in.

There are at least 15,000 kinds of protozoa. Probably there are many more. New ones are found from time to time. Two of the best known are the ameba and the little slipper animal, or paramecium. The ameba changes shape as it crawls about. It crawls by sending out tiny "false feet." To take in food, it simply moves over and around the particle of food. The paramecium swims fast by means of tiny hairlike pro-

There are many thousand kinds of protozoa but these tiny one-celled animals were almost unknown before the development of the microscope.

jections called cilia. Food comes into its body at only one place. Some protozoa are shaped like tiny flowers on stalks.

Tiny as they are, some protozoa have shells. The famous White Cliffs of Dover are made of chalk from countless billions of shells of certain protozoa.

Animals which are only a little more complicated than protozoa use protozoa as their food. In this way protozoa are helpful. But a few kinds of protozoa cause diseases. Malaria and sleeping sickness are two of the diseases they cause. (See AMEBA; CELL; CHALK; MALARIA; PARASITES.)

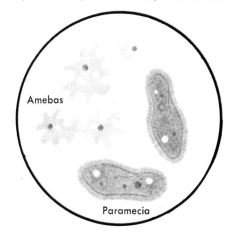

Amebas

Paramecia

PSYCHOLOGY How can pets be trained to do tricks? Why do some boys and girls have trouble learning to read? Why do some children always want to play by themselves? What makes some people behave so strangely that we say they have "lost their minds"?

Almost everyone has wondered at times about questions like these. It seems strange, then, that the science of psychology, which tries to answer such questions, is rather new—less than 100 years old. Psychology is often called the science of the mind. It deals with such things as memory, imagination, ability to think, emotions, and behavior.

Before the days of psychology there were some very wrong ideas about behavior. Evil spirits were often blamed for bad behavior. For centuries people believed in witches who could cast spells on people.

Another wrong idea was that the moon had some power over people's minds. A person who is mentally sick is sometimes called a "lunatic." "Lunatic" comes from *luna,* the Latin word for "moon."

Psychology is a big help in the study of mental illness. It helps in the study of other illness, too. Doctors are finding more and more that the mind and the rest of the body are very closely tied together. But psychology helps many people besides doctors. Because of it teachers know how to help boys and girls learn faster. Fathers and mothers are able to tell whether their children are making the progress they should. Employers are able to place the people they hire in the kinds of jobs best for them. Manufacturers know how to advertise their products. Lawyers and judges are helped in understanding the people with whom they deal.

So many people look to psychology for help that it is easy to see why it has many branches. A few of them are advertising psychology, child psychology, legal psychology, educational psychology, animal psychology, and medical psychology.

PUERTO RICO The island of Puerto Rico is an American land in the West Indies. It is about 1,000 miles from Florida. Puerto Rico became a possession of the United States in 1898 after a war with Spain. Today Puerto Rico is not a state. But Puerto Ricans have more independence than have any of the people of other outlying United States territories.

Columbus, on his second voyage to the New World, in 1493, discovered Puerto Rico. In 1508 the Spanish explorer Ponce de León founded the first settlement there. Later San Juan, now the capital city, became an important seaport of the Spanish Empire in the Americas. Spanish galleons bearing gold and silver anchored in its harbor before taking off for Spain. Sea captains like Sir Francis Drake came to San Juan to try to capture some of the treasure for the queen of England.

Today Puerto Rico is one of the most thickly peopled lands in the world. Over 2,000,000 people live on the small oblong island. For years most of them tried to make a living by farming. It was hard, and many Puerto Ricans were very poor.

Sugar cane is the chief money crop. Most of the thousands of sugar cane growers in Puerto Rico raise only a few tons apiece. The big production comes from a few large plantations on the lowlands near the coast. In the mountainous interior farmers raise tobacco and coffee. Tropical hurricanes often damage crops and add to the Puerto Rican farmers' problems.

Puerto Rican Flag

Tobacco

Coffee Beans

| Total population | 2,302,000 |
| Area (square miles) | 3,423 |

ELEVATION

Feet
2000 — 5000
1000 — 2000
0 — 1000

S   Sugar

Tobacco

Coffee

Textiles

R   Rum

F   Fruit

A few years ago Puerto Ricans started a program to make life on their tropical island better for themselves. More varied crops are now raised. There are jobs for many people in big new factories. Thousands of new homes have been built in large housing projects. Good highways, electric power plants, and new schools are among the things Puerto Ricans can now boast of. Puerto Rico, however, is still overcrowded and there is much poverty. Many Puerto Ricans leave the island to work in New York or other big American cities.

San Juan is the main port. At its docks men are busy loading bags of sugar on ships and unloading machinery and other products not yet made in Puerto Rican factories. San Juan has a big new airport.

Many visitors are among the passengers on planes from the United States. Guests enjoy the island's sea breezes, sandy beaches, and the comforts of its large hotels.

Puerto Ricans like to remember their Spanish background, and most of them speak Spanish. Many speak both Spanish and English. Visitors agree that Puerto Ricans are making their island a good place in which to live.

Chinese Shadow Puppet

Hand Position

Hand Puppet

Marionette Showing Body Joints and Strings

String Attachment of a Marionette

Marionette

PUPPETS One room in a famous restaurant in Chicago is a small theater. Every night an opera performance goes on in this theater. The music is on records. The actors are puppets. They move about the stage, wave their arms, dance, bow, and open their mouths. It is easy for the audience to imagine that the puppets are actually doing the singing.

There are four kinds of puppets. The four kinds are hand puppets, rod puppets, shadow puppets, and marionettes.

A hand puppet fits over a person's hand a little like a glove. The puppeteer makes the puppet go through its motions by moving his hand and fingers. The puppets that are used in Punch-and-Judy shows are usually hand puppets.

Rod puppets are worked with rods that reach up from below. The people of Java make beautiful puppets of this kind.

Shadow puppets are flat figures. The audience does not see the puppets themselves. It sees only their shadows on a screen. Shadow puppets are especially popular in China.

Marionettes are worked by means of strings from above. A marionette usually has at least three strings. It may have as many as 30. It takes a great deal of skill to manage a marionette well.

Puppets are not new. They have been found in ancient ruins in many places. In the Middle Ages they were very popular. Wandering showmen carried them to fairs and market places. A little more than 300 years ago the Puritans in England were very powerful. They thought that the plays being performed in the theaters had a bad influence on people. They closed all the theaters except puppet theaters. As a result, puppet theaters flourished.

In the United States no one was very much interested in puppets until about 1915. Since then there has been a great deal of interest. Puppets appear now on many television shows. Puppets are not always made to look like people. There are many puppets that look like dogs, horses, and dragons.

Famous writers and composers have written plays and music for puppet shows. And one of the best-liked of all children's stories is about a long-nosed puppet—Pinocchio—who is continually in trouble.

A strange thing happens when people watch puppets performing on a stage. The puppets are usually less than two feet tall. But when a person watches them perform they come to seem life-size. Tony Sarg made himself famous with his puppets in the 1920's. He and his puppets traveled about the country giving plays. At the end of a play Tony Sarg himself would appear on the stage. Everyone would gasp. He looked like a real giant.

Working with puppets is a rather common hobby. Many boys and girls have fun making puppets and writing plays for them. (See HOBBIES; THEATER.)

PYGMIES The Pygmies live in the jungles of Africa. Since they never grow to be tall, they are sometimes called "the jungle's little children." They have some close relatives in the jungles of the South Sea Islands and southeastern Asia.

The tallest Pygmies do not measure much over four and a half feet. Their heads, mouths, and noses are broad, and their legs are short. They are dark-skinned but are not as dark as Negroes. As a rule they are brave, carefree, and happy.

Pygmies live in tribes headed by chiefs. The members of a tribe are very loyal to one another. They fight for one another and share food. Their homes are huts made of branches and leaves.

Meat is the most important food of the Pygmies. They catch wild animals with traps and spears. The traps are deep holes covered with branches of trees and other green plants. In them elephants, okapi, hippopotamuses, giant hogs, and leopards are caught. After an animal is caught, the Pygmies kill it with spears. The tips of the spears are dipped in a vegetable poison. Pygmies sometimes kill gorillas with their poison spears. One Pygmy will trick a gorilla by running and letting the gorilla chase him. When the gorilla is almost upon him the Pygmy pretends to stumble. As he does so, he drives his spear into the ground, point up and slanted toward the gorilla. Plants hide the spear. The gorilla rushes against it and is killed. The hunter then gives a cry and other Pygmies join him to enjoy a feast.

Some Pygmies have worked out a kind of silent trading with their taller neighbors. They take vegetables and fruit from the neighbors' gardens and leave meat as payment. Sometimes they shoot an arrow into a bunch of bananas they are planning to come back later to take. They are too shy to trade in the ordinary way.

Pygmies cannot write or read. But they have ways of sending messages. They form their love messages by sewing seeds and beads on pieces of soft hide.

Some Pygmies dress up more than others. Some wear very fancy headdresses of horns, feathers, beads, or eggshells. (See RACES OF MAN; SAVAGES.)

Daring Pygmy hunters often kill gorillas.

Slaves toiled many years to build the pyramids.

PYRAMIDS On the great rocky plain of Giza in Egypt stand three of the world's most remarkable buildings—three pyramids. There are many other pyramids in Egypt, but these three are the largest and most famous. It is thrilling to think that these buildings have lasted for more than 4,000 years. Great cities have been built and have fallen into ruins while the pyramids have stood. As an Arab proverb says, they "mock time."

These biggest pyramids have been called artificial mountains. The tallest is as tall as a 40-story building. Its base is bigger than an ordinary city block.

The pyramids were tombs of Egyptian rulers. The Egyptians believed in life after death. Each ruler had many of his treasures buried with him so that in the after-world, his spirit could enjoy them. The pyramids were built large to last a long time and to tell the world how great the rulers were. They were built large also in order to safeguard each ruler's mummy and his treasures.

The rooms inside the pyramids are very small. The buildings are chiefly solid stone. It took millions of blocks of stone for a big pyramid. Many of the blocks weighed more than a ton apiece. These great tombs were built long before the days of big machines. The wonder is that the blocks of stone could be moved long distances and be put in place. A big pyramid meant the work of thousands of slaves for many years.

Other amazing things about the pyramids are that the stones are fitted together very skilfully, and that the measurements are very exact. The four sides of the greatest pyramid come within inches of measuring exactly the same. In fact this greatest pyramid—the pyramid of King Khufu—is such a marvel of building that it is one of the seven wonders of the world. (See EGYPT; MUMMIES; SEVEN WONDERS OF THE WORLD.)

PLACE	RULER	BASE FEET	HEIGHT FEET
Saqqara	Djoser 2700 B. C.	394 x 355	196
Dahshur	Snefru 2650 B. C.	624	328
	Unknown	722	324
Maidum	Snefru 2650 B. C.	475	301
Giza	Khufu 2600 B. C.	755	481
	Khaf-Re 2560 B. C.	708	472
	Men-kau-Re 2525 B. C.	357	219

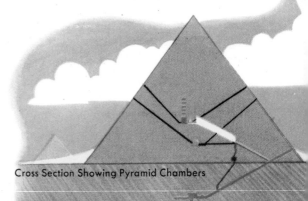

Cross Section Showing Pyramid Chambers

The letter Q came from this letter in the earliest alphabet: ∞ . Perhaps it was the picture of a looped rope, perhaps of a stomach. The Phoenicians made the letter like this: φ . The Greeks changed it somewhat (φ). They soon found that they did not need the letter in writing their language, but they kept it as the sign for 90. The Romans made it a letter again (Q). This is the way it has come down to us.

In English words Q is always followed by U. Qu sometimes stands for a "k" sound, as in *unique*. It sometimes has a *kw* sound instead, as in *quiet* and *quick*.

QUAGGA A hundred and fifty years ago there were great herds of quaggas in Africa. Now there are not any at all there or anywhere else. Too many were killed for their meat and their hides. One quagga

The quagga is now extinct.

lived in the London Zoo for years after all the other quaggas had disappeared. But it died many years ago.

The quaggas were cousins of the horses and the zebras and the wild asses. As the picture shows, in some ways a quagga looked very much like a zebra. But it was not hard to tell these two animals apart. The quagga had stripes, but they were on only the front part of its body. Besides, the quagga was striped light brown and dark brown instead of black and white. Its tail had much more hair than a zebra's.

Early settlers in South Africa tried to tame quaggas. But they were no easier to tame than zebras. Farmers could not train quaggas to pull plows or wagons, but they did find them useful in one way. The farmers sometimes, it is said, kept quaggas with their herds of cattle to protect the cattle from hyenas. The quaggas killed the hyenas with their hard hoofs.

A quagga neighed just as zebras and horses do. But its neigh sounded like a bark. Its odd name came from the sound it made. (See HORSES; HYENA; ZEBRA.)

QUAIL We think of birds as flying creatures, but many birds spend most of their lives on the ground. The quail in the picture is one of them. This quail is often called the bobwhite. It gets the name from its cheery call of "bobwhite, bobwhite."

Bobwhite families are large. From 10 to 18 eggs are laid in a nest in the grass. Bobwhite babies are covered with down when they are hatched and can run about almost

The bobwhite, or quail, is a game bird.

at once. When very young, they look much like baby chickens.

Bobwhites do not go south for the winter, as many birds do. They remain in family groups called coveys. The birds of a covey stay close together during the daytime as they hunt for food. If an enemy comes close, the covey breaks up and the birds fly away with a loud whirr of wings. They scatter in all directions. But they do not fly far or high above the ground. Soon they can be heard whistling their name as they try to get together again. To sleep, the birds of a covey arrange themselves in a circle with their heads facing out.

No bird is a better friend of the farmer than the bobwhite. It eats both weed seeds and harmful insects.

The meat of the bobwhite is very good to eat. This helpful bird might soon disappear if there were no laws to protect it.

In America there are several other kinds of quail. There are quail in the Old World, too. Some of them migrate. The Bible tells that flights of quail helped save the Israelites from starvation as they wandered in the wilderness some 32 centuries ago. (See BIRDS; GAME BIRDS.)

QUAKERS About 300 years ago in England a new religious group was formed. The group called itself the Society of Friends. Their leader was George Fox. At first the Friends were badly treated simply because their religion was different from that of their neighbors. Many Friends were thrown into prison. In court one day Fox told the magistrate that he should "tremble at the word of the Lord." "Tremble" and "quake" mean the same. People began calling the Friends "Quakers."

At first people called the Friends "Quakers" to make fun of them. But no one calls them Quakers now to make fun of them. They have won good will the world over.

Since the early Quakers were badly treated in England, it is not surprising that many of them came to America. But in some of the American colonies they were badly treated, too. Rhode Island, however, welcomed them. Then William Penn sent a band of Quakers from England to found a Quaker colony. It became the state of Pennsylvania. Today there are Quakers in all parts of the United States.

Quakers believe in living simple lives. The early Quakers wore gray costumes like

Friends' Meetinghouse

Modern Quakers

Quakers of the 1800's

those pictured. Now Quakers no longer wear costumes, but they do not believe in showy or fancy clothes.

When several people sit in a group without talking, someone may say that they are having a "Quaker meeting." For Quaker services are very simple. In most of them there is no preacher, no choir, and no organist. The group sits quietly until someone wishes to speak. Everyone, young or old, has a right to speak in a meeting.

A Quaker can sometimes be told by his way of talking. He may use "thee" instead of "you" in talking with friends.

Quakers do not believe in fighting, even for their country. But they play their part in wartime. In both World War I and World War II they did very important relief work. They could do this work because even the enemy trusted them.

In peacetime, too, the Quakers do much to help others. The American Friends Service Committee works in North America, Central America, Europe, and Asia. The work camps it carries on give young people a wonderful chance to be helpful.

The Quakers believe strongly in education. In the United States they have several colleges and many other schools. Through their teachings the Quakers are helping people understand that peoples of all races and religions are brothers.

QUARRYING In many places it is easy to find a piece of granite or limestone the size of a marble or even the size of a man's hand. Such pieces have been washed or worked out of the ground and are found scattered far and wide. But pieces of these rocks big enough to use in building a big building are not easy to find. As a rule, pieces of rock big enough for buildings have to be dug out of the earth.

Digging such rocks out of the ground is called quarrying. Granite and limestone are not the only rocks that are quarried. Among the others that are quarried are marble, slate, and sandstone.

Ridges show where the marble has been cut out.

Limestone, slate, and sandstone are more easily quarried than granite and marble because they are formed in layers. Huge pieces are split off by drills. The pieces can be broken apart between the layers. Granite must be cut into blocks. So must marble.

Quarrying is not new. Granite quarries at Aswan in Egypt have been furnishing building stone for more than 4300 years. Perhaps even older are the limestone quarries across the Nile from Giza, where the great pyramids stand.

A big problem in early quarrying was moving the stone that was cut. Yet for the Great Pyramid of Khufu the Egyptians moved six and a quarter million tons of stone. The separate blocks averaged about two and a half tons apiece. The Nile River helped. At flood time the blocks of stone could be floated part of the way. Slaves did the rest. Fortunately in quarrying today huge machines take the place of slaves. (See BUILDING MATERIALS.)

Blocks of limestone are raised with a derrick.

QUARTZ The mineral quartz is one of the commonest substances in the world. Most grains of sand are tiny bits of quartz. Grains of sand are formed by the breaking up of rocks. Quartz is a part of many different kinds of rock.

The scientists' shorthand way of writing quartz is SiO_2. This sign tells that quartz is made of silicon and oxygen.

Quartz is the hardest of all the common minerals. It is not as hard as diamond or ruby or topaz, but they are not common. If diamond, the hardest of all substances, is given a grade of ten for hardness, the grade of quartz is seven. Quartz will scratch all other common minerals.

Quartz is often found in the form of beautiful crystals. They have six sides. Their ends are six-sided pyramids.

Pure quartz is colorless. It is clearer than glass. Often it is called rock crystal. The crystal balls of the old-time astrologers were made of rock crystal. The ancient Greeks thought that rock crystal was water frozen so hard that it would never melt. The queer lumps of stone called geodes (JEE odes) often have beautiful pure quartz crystals inside.

A very great deal of the quartz in the world is not pure. It has in it impurities that color it and, as a rule, keep it from being transparent. The impurities in it may make quartz more beautiful than clear rock crystal.

Some impure quartz comes in large crystals. Some is glassy but does not form in separate crystals. In some quartz there are crystals too tiny and crowded together to be seen without a microscope.

Amethyst is violet colored quartz. Citrine is yellow quartz. Blue quartz, of course, is blue, and smoky quartz has a smoky look. These varieties of quartz come in crystals. Amethyst and citrine are cut into stones for jewelry.

Rose quartz is a lovely pink. It is not found in separate crystals but in masses. This quartz makes beautiful beads.

Agate, onyx, and bloodstone are varieties of quartz in which the crystals are too small to be seen without a microscope. They may be beautifully colored.

But not all quartz is beautiful. Flint, for instance, is impure quartz. Our early ancestors found it very useful for arrowheads, but no one uses it for jewelry.

Today we use quartz not only for decoration but in many other ways. Sheets of rock crystal are important parts of radio, television, and radar transmitters. It is used for lenses in telescopes and moving picture projectors. Its big advantage here is that it does not crack or change size when it is heated or cooled.

Pure quartz can be melted and made into sheets that look like glass. It is then called fused quartz. Fused quartz will let ultraviolet light go through it; glass will not. Fused quartz is therefore used in the windows of some hospitals and in some of the special kinds of lamps doctors use. It is used in making "glassware" for chemists. Even hot acid will not dissolve it. The "sand" of some sandpaper is quartz sand. Great quantities of quartz go into the making of glass. This mineral comes into our lives in more ways than most of us guess. (See CARBORUNDUM; CRYSTALS; GEMS; JEWELRY; MINERALS; ROCKS; SAND.)

TYPES OF QUARTZ

Blue Quartz

Amethyst

Citrine

Smoky Quartz

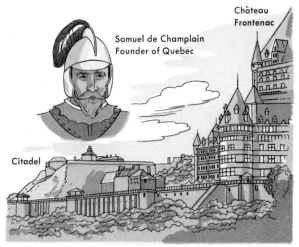

Samuel de Champlain
Founder of Quebec

Château Frontenac

Citadel

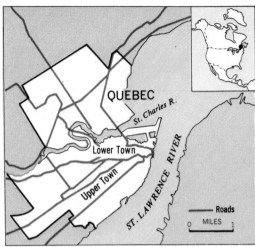

QUEBEC

St. Charles R.

Lower Town

Upper Town

ST. LAWRENCE RIVER

Roads

0 MILES 1

QUEBEC The St. Lawrence River reaches far into North America from the Atlantic Ocean. This river served as a highway for early French explorers. One of them was Samuel de Champlain. Eight hundred miles from the Atlantic the St. Lawrence suddenly narrows. Here on the northern bank in 1608 Champlain founded a French settlement. He called it Quebec. Now Quebec is one of Canada's great cities. Its name comes from an Algonquin Indian word meaning the "place where the river narrows."

Part of Quebec is built on low land along the river. Part of the city is on a high tableland. The highest part is called Cape Diamond. It is 350 feet above the river. There is a public elevator that carries people up and down between the two sections of the city.

Just as part of Quebec is high and part low, part of it is old with narrow, winding streets, and part is new and modern with broad avenues. About 150 years ago the English, who by that time were the rulers of Canada, built a wall around the city. Although the city has spread far beyond it, the wall still stands. Quebec is the only walled city in North America.

The picture shows two of Quebec's famous buildings. The Château Frontenac, which looks like a French castle, is a hotel. The Citadel is an old English fort.

Canada is divided into provinces just as the United States is divided into states. The city of Quebec is the capital of the province of Quebec.

Many of the people of both the city and the province of Quebec are descendants of the early French settlers there. French is the language most commonly used over most of the province.

Quebec is one of Canada's great ports. It is not as important a port as Montreal, which is also on the St. Lawrence, but to its docks come ships from all over the world. They get cargoes of lumber, grain, and asbestos. The lumber comes from the forests near by. The grain is brought from the great plains of middle Canada. The asbestos is mined in the eastern part of Canada. Shipping can be carried on for only eight or nine months a year. For the other months the river is frozen.

Shipbuilding and papermaking are two of the kinds of work by which the people of Quebec earn their living. The forests near at hand furnish the wood needed for both ships and paper.

For Americans a visit to Quebec is much like a visit to Europe. It is not surprising that every year tourists go from the United States by the thousands to this interesting Canadian city. (See ASBESTOS; CANADA; MONTREAL; ST. LAWRENCE RIVER.)

QUETZAL The quetzal is a beautiful bird that is found in the forests of Central America and Mexico. It is even more beautiful, many people think, than the bird of paradise. A male quetzal is as bright-colored as a parrot. And it has two plumes in its tail that may be more than a yard long.

In the days before the conquering Spaniards came to the New World, the Aztecs and Mayas thought that the quetzal was sacred. Only rulers and priests could wear its feathers. A person could be put to death for killing a quetzal.

Now the quetzal is the national bird of Guatemala. It stands for freedom to the people of that country just as the eagle stands for freedom to the people of the United States. Some of the coins of Guatemala have a quetzal on them. In fact, one Guatemalan coin is called a quetzal.

Quetzals build their nests in old woodpecker holes. They make the holes larger with their strong beaks.

These birds are hard to keep in captivity. It is hard to make them eat anything. In the forests where they live they eat fruit of a certain kind that grows there. A quetzal picks a fruit and flies to a perch on a tree before swallowing the fruit. It takes a great deal of patience to make a quetzal change its eating habits. Perhaps the quetzal came to stand for freedom because it cannot easily be kept in a cage. (See AZTECS; BIRDS OF PARADISE; MAYAS; PARROTS AND PARAKEETS.)

QUICKSAND Grains of sand usually have sharp edges. When they are wet, they pack together. It is easy to walk on wet sand of the ordinary kind. Even automobiles can travel over it easily.

But in some beds of sand the grains are tiny and round and smooth. When these grains are wet, they do not pack together. They roll over one another almost as if they were water, and quickly swallow up anything heavy that rests on them. Sand of this kind is called quicksand.

Men and horses and cattle have been lost in quicksand. Once a whole freight train was swallowed up.

Quicksand may be at the surface of the ground. It may be down below the surface. The men who dig tunnels dread quicksand. If they strike quicksand it may rush into the tunnel and fill it up before they have a chance to stop it.

Quicksand is most likely to be found in the parts of the world that were covered with ice during the great Ice Age. The ice, as it moved along, ground off the rough edges of the grains of sand. It is most likely to be found, too, where there is a layer of clay under the sand. The layer of clay does not let water sink through it easily. The water stays in the sand above. No sand is quicksand unless it is wet. (See CAISSON; SAND.)

Quicksand is a hazard to cattle on the range.